DISCOVERY & EXPLORATION

Exploration in
the Age of Empire
1750–1953

KEVIN PATRICK GRANT

JOHN S. BOWMAN and MAURICE ISSERMAN
General Editors

Facts On File, Inc.

For Wouter Germans

Exploration in the Age of Empire, 1750–1953

Copyright © 2005 by Kevin Patrick Grant
Captions copyright © 2005 by Facts On File, Inc.
Maps © 2005 by Facts On File, Inc.

Facts On File, Inc.
132 West 31st Street
New York NY 10001

Library of Congress Cataloging-in-Publication Data

Grant, Kevin.
    Exploration in the age of empire, 1750–1953 / Kevin Patrick Grant.
      v. cm. —(Discovery and exploration)
    Includes bibliographical references (p.) and index.
    Contents: "Dr. Livingstone, I presume?"—The modern era of exploration and
empire—The great game in Central Asia—Following the Niger and the Nile—
Taming the Heart of Darkness—Pilgrimages to Mecca and the Arabian sands—
Exploring the top of the world.
    ISBN 0-8160-5260-3
    1. Discoveries in geography—European—Juvenile literature. [1. Discoveries
in geography—European. 2. Explorers.] I. Title. II. Series.
    G133.G67 2004
    910'.94'0903—dc22   2003025847

Text design by Erika K. Arroyo
Cover design by Pehrsson Design
Maps by Sholto Ainslie, Patricia Meschino, and Dale Williams

Printed in the United States of America

VB FOF 10 9 8 7 6 5 4 3 2 1

This book is printed on acid-free paper.

Contents

NOTE ON PHOTOS

Many of the illustrations and photographs used in this book are old, historical images. The quality of the prints is not always up to current standards, as in some cases the originals are from old or poor quality negatives or are damaged. The content of the illustrations, however, made their inclusion important despite problems in reproduction.

INTRODUCTION

Historians commonly refer to the "New World" that Christopher Columbus encountered in 1492, but one must remember that this encounter was the product of European forces and desires that had existed for centuries. Europe's monarchies had long wanted to build their wealth and extend the reach of Christianity, both to please their God and to secure their borders against each other and the powerful Islamic kingdoms to the east and the south. It had been hundreds of years since the borders of the Roman Empire had fallen back from Asia and the Holy Lands, the region that is now called the Middle East. At the beginning of the 15th century, Europe was besieged by Islamic kingdoms and frustrated in its attempts to find reliable trade routes through the Holy Lands to Cathay, present-day China. This would all begin to change by the end of the 15th century, however, when Europeans simultaneously pushed back the Islamic powers to the south and encountered the Americas, opening the way for Europe's westward expansion. This book examines the European exploration of the world in this new age of empire.

The general purpose of this book is to demonstrate how exploration was driven and influenced by European empires, and how exploration responded to changes in these empires between the 16th and 20th centuries. This book focuses on the period after the 18th century and on explorations in Asia, Africa, and the Middle East. Europeans had made their initial explorations of these regions by the 16th century, but it was only after the 18th century, under the influence of intense imperial competition, that Europeans thoroughly explored these regions and then, in many cases, established their control. Exploration after the 18th century played an essential role in establishing a global system of European empires that would endure until the middle decades of the 20th century, when it finally gave way to nationalist movements for independence.

This book has three major themes that bring together the wide-ranging, and generally uncoordinated, experiences of exploration around the world. The first thematic subject is motive. Why did explorers leave hearth and home to risk everything in uncharted waters, in unmapped jungles, or on snow-covered, windswept mountains? When asked in 1923 why he wanted to climb Mount Everest, George Mallory replied, "Because it is there." He saw in Everest an epic challenge, and a year later he died on the mountain in his attempt to meet that challenge. There is no doubt that many others, like Mallory, were drawn to the challenge and the adventure of exploration. Yet people also undertook explorations with specific material and moral objectives in mind. They went in search of personal fortunes in gold and silver, or in search of opportunities to trade in foreign markets. They searched for sea routes or lands that would provide strategic advantage over imperial adversaries. They set out to advance scientific understanding, or to save souls by spreading the Christian faith. There were many motives for exploration, and the particular power of each motive must be understood in the historical context in which it was conceived.

The second theme of this book is how changing ideas influenced the conduct and understanding of exploration. How were the perspectives of explorers shaped by the most influential ideas of their periods? How did the observations of explorers reflect these ideas? An important shift occurred between the ideas of the Europeans who encountered the Americas in the 15th century and the ideas of the Europeans who extended Europe's overseas empires after the 18th century. The former were influenced by the Renaissance, an era of intellectual and artistic innovation in Europe. While artists such as Leonardo da Vinci attempted to perfect the portrayal of the individual human form, scholars used their individual powers of reason to question common beliefs about subjects ranging from astronomy to the principles of Christianity. European intellectuals and artists of the 18th century also attempted to use reason to extend the boundaries of knowledge, but with greater reliance on scientific methods. While Europeans generally maintained their belief in a Christian God, the Enlightenment pro-

moted scientific objectivity that produced new ideas about such subjects as government and economics. As exploration continued during the 19th and 20th centuries, Europeans' perspectives would additionally reflect new ideas about race and foreign cultures; ideas produced by developments in both the natural and social sciences. In the early 15th century, explorers described new lands filled with heathens and marvels. By the 20th century, explorers regarded new lands as places to be measured and understood with scientific instruments.

The last major theme of this book is the way in which the competition and politics of European empires shaped, and were shaped by, exploration. What were the potential strategic and economic advantages that induced imperial governments to support explorations from the Niger River in West Africa to the Himalayan Mountains of Tibet? When and how did exploration become a source of national pride? This book discusses how the changing balance of military power influenced exploration after the 18th century, and how industrialization drove explorers into the center of Africa in search of raw materials for products such as chocolate candy and bicycle tires. Great Britain was the dominant military and industrial power in the world by the late 18th century, and it became the dominant imperial power for the next 150 years—over most of the period that is the main subject of this book. In the 19th century, Great Britain produced explorers who became national heroes, and, in some cases, international celebrities. Britain was not alone in this, as one will see in the chapters that follow. In fact, exploration became an extension of national pride, and national rivalry, that would continue to play out even on the slopes of Mount Everest in the mid-20th century, as the era of Europe's overseas empires came to a close.

This book offers an account of exploration that is both traditional in its general organization and innovative in its particular attention to the context of empire. It recounts the experiences and achievements of individual explorers, while incorporating developments in the scholarship on exploration in recent decades. Most historical studies of exploration continue to use a traditional narrative that follows the individual explorer through adversity to success or noble failure. The best work of this kind takes a broader view on the context of the explorer's life and uses a variety of documentary sources to illuminate many facets of the individual's character. The heroic narrative of exploration has traditionally been a narrative of progress, but this perspective has been called into question in recent decades, as some historians of exploration have begun to take a more critical perspective. For example, Alan Moorehead argues in his book *The Fatal Impact: The Invasion of the South Pacific, 1767–1840* that European exploration in the Pacific did tremendous damage to the societies and cultures of the Pacific Islanders. This change in perspective on the history of exploration was primarily caused by increased awareness about, and sensitivity to, the often terrible price that explorers exacted from the peoples who they encountered in the Americas, the Pacific, and elsewhere. Whether indigenous peoples were afflicted by the explorer's own brutality or by the diseases that the explorer unwittingly carried, their experience of suffering and social crisis has been difficult to reconcile with a heroic story of progress. This conflict between the histories of exploration was most clearly manifested in 1992, when the 500th anniversary of Columbus's encounter with the Americas was greeted with both celebrations and political protests.

There have been other developments in the history of exploration. Whereas biographies of explorers once focused upon men, there has been over the past 25 years a growing number of works published by and about women explorers. For example, there is Jane Fletcher Geniesse's biography *Passionate Nomad: The Life of Freya Stark*, which chronicles the remarkable experiences of a woman who lived among the tribes of the Syrian desert. Recently, historians have also begun to discuss the indigenous guides, translators, and porters who were essential to the work of European exploration, as one finds in Frank McLynn, *Hearts of Darkness*. Academic historians and scientists have furthermore turned their attention beyond particular explorers to consider broader, related issues, such as technology and ecology. Some fine works of this kind are Jared Diamond's *Guns, Germs, and Steel* and Alfred Crosby's *Ecological Imperialism*. Finally, an increasing amount of work is being done on what one might call the cultures of exploration—that is, the ways in which Europeans understood and responded to exploration, particularly after the middle of the 19th century. In 1996, for instance, the British National Portrait Gallery in London staged an exhibition about the missionary and explorer Dr. David Livingstone, which said as much about Victorian England as it did about the explorer himself. The exhibition was accompanied by a beautifully illustrated catalog, *David Livingstone and the Victorian Encounter with Africa*. The book at hand reflects these various developments in the history of exploration, bringing them to bear upon the general relationship between exploration and empire.

The text of this book is enlivened by the observations and opinions of the explorers themselves, conveyed in their own words through memoirs and travel narratives. The text is complemented by maps that illuminate different regions of Asia, Africa, and the Middle East, and the explorers' particular routes through them. There are illustrations, including drawings, paintings, and photographs, which portray the explorers, their equipment, and their means of travel, from canoes to camels. The text is also complemented by in-depth essays on related topics of particular interest, including the threat of the tsetse fly in tropical Africa and the development of oxygen technology for mountain climbers at extreme altitudes in the Himalayas. A comprehensive glossary of special or unusual terms provides assistance to the reader in following explorers through many environments and cultures around the world. The book then concludes by providing the reader with a rich variety of sources that offer further information on exploration and European empires in Asia, Africa, and the Middle East.

1

"Dr. Livingstone, I Presume?"

 Dr. David Livingstone, the most famous British explorer of the 19th century, had grown impatient on the banks of the Lualaba River in central Africa. For three months he had watched the river flow slowly northward into the heart of Africa, and he had looked westward across the two-mile expanse of the river to the distant shore. He was desperate to cross the river, as he believed that on the other side he would discover four miraculous fountains that would prove to be the source of the great Nile River to the north. Unfortunately, Livingstone and his 13 African servants had been unable to persuade anyone in the local town of Nyangwe to take them across the river in canoes. It was July 15, 1871, and Livingstone had already made his final offer—or, more accurately, he had offered everything that he had to give. He had told a man named Dugumbe, one of the leading merchants in the town, that he would give him the then-astronomical sum of $2,000 and all the supplies he had stored in the distant town of Ujiji for passage across the river.

With this offer on the table, Livingstone decided to pass the time in the town's marketplace, where more than a thousand people had come to haggle over fruits and vegetables, fish and livestock, earthenware pots, and other odds and ends. After about an hour, Livingstone began to make his way out of the market, owing to the sultry heat of the day, when he noticed three men, armed with guns, arguing with one of the local African merchants over the price of a chicken. The armed men were not from Nyangwe—rather, they were Muslims from East Africa, commonly known to Europeans of the day as Arabs. These men were in Nyangwe under the authority of Dugumbe, a fellow Arab, to profit from the slave trade and from blood feuds between Dugumbe and his adversaries. "Before I had got thirty yards out," Livingstone later recalled in his journal, "the discharge of two guns in the middle of the crowd told me that slaughter had begun: crowds dashed off from the place, and threw down their wares in confusion, and ran." The three armed men opened fire upon the fleeing crowd, and another group of armed Arabs joined in shooting at the men and women who attempted to scramble to a nearby creek and escape in their canoes. When the many panic-stricken people became jammed in the small creek, hundreds jumped into the river and began to swim for an island about a mile off-shore. Livingstone watched the long line of heads bobbing in the water, and he realized with horror that the current would carry them well beyond the island and then downstream, where most would surely drown. "Shot after shot continued to be fired on the helpless and perishing," Livingstone recalled in his journal. "Some of the long line of heads disappeared quietly; while other poor creatures threw their arms high and sank. One canoe took in as many as it could hold, and all paddled with hands and arms: three canoes, got out in haste, picked up sinking friends, till all went down together and disappeared."

The people of Nyangwe had fled the market to escape enslavement. Many had assumed that the armed men intended to round them up, place them in chains and wooden collars, then march them to the coast to be sold. For some, given a choice, even death was preferable to enslavement, or so it seemed to Livingstone. He watched a woman in the river refuse to be rescued by men who Dugumbe had dispatched in canoes. The woman drowned, as Livingstone stood help-lessly on the shore.

DR. LIVINGSTONE'S DILEMMA

The slave trade in central Africa was flourish-ing in the mid-19th century, as it had for many years. On the Lualaba River, the trade was dominated by Muslims from the east, who abducted or purchased from local chiefs the

Bantu peoples of the region. The slave traders then sold these people to work on coastal plantations, which specialized in the produc-tion of cloves, or to be shipped to the Arabian Peninsula and Asia, where the Africans were sold again to work as manual laborers or ser-vants. The coastal and overseas trade in slaves had become more difficult since the British government had abolished the slave trade and emancipated slaves throughout much of the British Empire in 1833. By mid-century, the British Royal Navy had a special Anti-Slavery Squadron that patrolled the African coasts, intercepting slave ships. On the east coast, the squadron primarily targeted Arab slave traders, and on the west coast it primarily tar-geted the Portuguese, the dominant slave traders in the Atlantic. Ironically, as the British government pursued its antislavery policies, British and other European explorers de-pended in many respects upon the slave trade for their survival and their discoveries. They followed the age-old routes of the slave cara-vans, and they often relied on the advice and support of the same slave traders whose work they condemned.

Livingstone had begun his career in explo-ration as a "medical missionary" of the Lon-don Missionary Society (LMS), combining his skills as a physician with his efforts to convert Africans to Christianity. He had then become an abolitionist, as opponents of slavery were then known. He was following in the footsteps of his wife's father, Robert Moffat, who had been a famous missionary and abolitionist in South Africa. From the outset of his own work in Africa, Livingstone had regarded explo-ration as essential to the success of his Christ-ian mission on the grounds that it would forge the path for Christian civilization to follow. He had then come to believe that exploration was essential to exposing the horrors of the slave trade. After many years, he had determined

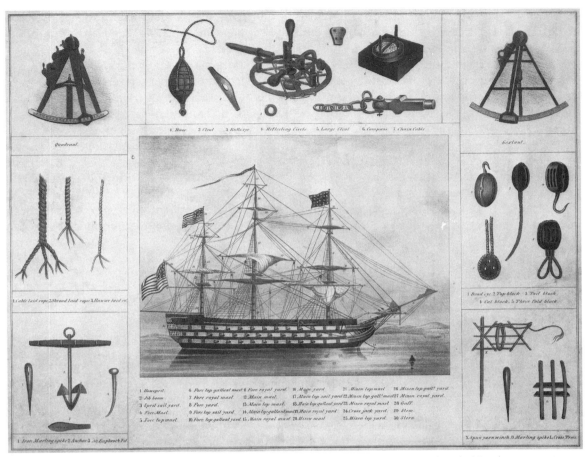

Ships were integral to life in the mid-19th century. The one in this engraving, surrounded by its equipment, could have carried anything from explorers traveling from Britain to Africa, to slaves being transported to the colonies in America. *(Library of Congress, Prints and Photographs Division [LC-USZC4-1942])*

that exploration must be his primary task, so he had left his missionary society to become a British consular official, with general instructions to report on slavery in Africa. This emissary of exploration and empire would subsequently report the massacre at Nyangwe to the British Foreign Office, provoking official and popular outrage in Britain that led to further government action against the African slave trade. In the meantime, however, Livingstone faced a moral dilemma. Was it right for him to depend upon Dugumbe and other slave traders for his progress to the four fountains, the legendary source of the Nile?

In response to the massacre at Nyangwe, Livingstone decided to give up his attempts to cross the Lualaba, if only for the time being. He prepared to return to his base of operations at Ujiji, on the shores of Lake Tanganyika, where he hoped to muster a new company of servants to accompany him in his explorations. There is no doubt that Dugumbe and the other slave traders in the vicinity were pleased to see Livingstone go. They knew that he had won support for his explorations in Britain by promising to investigate and expose the ongoing slave trade in Africa. Although the slave traders had helped Livingstone to survive in the jungles of Africa, they had also refused to deliver his consular reports and letters via their caravans to the coast. Now, as Livingstone prepared to depart in the aftermath of the massacre, Dugumbe gave him gunpowder and other necessities for the jour-

ney in a gesture of good faith. Livingstone accepted the supplies and left Nyangwe on July 22, 1871.

In the next several weeks, Livingstone and his African servants covered hundreds of miles of difficult terrain, walking paths only as wide as a man's outstretched arms, between walls of dense jungle foliage that rose vertically on either side to hide the light of day. Livingstone had several bouts of fever, and he steadily lost weight during the march. In a dangerous case of mistaken identity, African villagers thought that Livingstone was a slave trader and attempted to kill him in retaliation

Abolition and Exploration

The trans-Atlantic trade in African slaves had begun in the 16th century, when the Spanish and Portuguese shipped people from West Africa to South America to work on their colonial plantations and mines. Opposition to slavery increased in Europe in the 18th century under the influence of evangelical Protestant Christianity, the Enlightenment, and changing ideas about economics. The British government was the first to abolish the slave trade after 1807, and then in 1833 it declared slavery itself to be illegal in the British Empire. This was a momentous decision because Britain possessed the most extensive overseas empire of any European nation. The British Royal Navy then followed this decision by deploying an Anti-Slavery Squadron to patrol the African coasts, looking for slave traders.

It soon became clear, however, that the British government could not simply end slavery with the stroke of the pen. Government investigations in the 1830s discovered that conditions equivalent to slavery still existed in the British Caribbean. Moreover, the European owners of the plantation system in the Americas responded to British opposition by moving their operations closer to the source of their slave labor. After the early 19th century, slave plantations grew on both the west and east coasts of Africa. Also, the slave trade continued to feed the slave systems in the United States, in the colonies of Spain, Portugal, and France, and in the Middle East and Asia. The continuation of the slave trade in the era of emancipation was not lost upon British humanitarians, such as Livingstone, who justified exploration in Africa as an essential part of the campaign for abolition. The idea that exploration served the cause of abolition was later taken up by many European governments as a means to justify for the slave trader's previous brutality. In dense jungle, a spear flew closely behind Livingstone and stuck in the ground. Further down the trail, a spear flew just a foot in front of him, prompting Livingstone and his servants to shoot blindly into the jungle, to no apparent affect. Despite these and other mishaps along the way, Livingstone arrived at Ujiji on October 23. He appeared—by his own account—"a skeleton."

Livingstone had planned to buy the services of porters at Ujiji, or, if necessary, to wait to hire men who would eventually arrive with caravans from the coast. Unfortunately, before he could make any such arrangements, one of his employees betrayed him and sold most of his supplies, turning a profit at Livingstone's expense. The people of Ujiji would not help Livingstone recover his supplies, so he was powerless. Moreover, Livingstone could not count on the British government for help. The nearest consular officials were hundreds of miles away on the east coast, and neither these officials nor any other Europeans knew of Livingstone's precise location. There was not a white man in Africa who had seen Livingstone in the previous two years, and it had been many months since any of his letters had

imperial expansion into Africa. King Leopold II of Belgium became a vocal advocate of exploration and abolition in the 1870s. All the major European imperial powers then committed themselves to abolishing slavery in Africa under the Declaration of the Berlin Conference in 1885.

While Britain possessed the most extensive overseas empire of any European nation, their abolition of the slave trade, and then slavery itself after 1833, did not immediately end the practice. The slave trade continued through the 19th century, and slavery continues to exist to this day in parts of Africa, such as Sudan. *(Library of Congress, Prints and Photographs Division [LC-USZ62-108399])* reached the coast. In fact, long before Livingstone struggled back to Ujiji, rumors had begun to circulate in Europe and the United States that the great explorer was either lost or dead.

Isolated and in poor health, Livingstone was forced to live on the charity of his hosts. "This was distressing," Livingstone observed in his journal. "To wait in beggary was what I never contemplated, and I now felt miserable." It was not clear when, if ever, Livingstone would again have a chance to find the source of the Nile, and it was not even clear how long he would be welcome at Ujiji, a town established and dominated by slave traders. Under these difficult circumstances, on another morning of bleak prospects, Livingstone saw his servant, Abdullah Susi, running toward him with some urgent news. "An Englishman," Susi declared, "I see him!" And the young man then dashed away.

PURSUING THE RUMOR OF LIVINGSTONE

Henry Morton Stanley had crested a ridge and seen Lake Tanganyika and the port of Ujiji some 500 yards below. He was not an Englishman, but an American journalist who had been commissioned by a newspaper, the *New York Herald*, to lead an expedition into central Africa to determine whether the famous Dr. Livingstone was, in fact, dead or alive. Stanley had departed from the East African coast almost eight months before, at the head of a caravan of almost 200 African men. He and his followers had fought numerous battles against hostile tribes and nearly starved in the course of their arduous march. Stanley had overcome a mutiny, and he had survived 23 attacks of fever, all while navigating his way through the African jungle in pursuit of a rumor that Livingstone was at Lake Tan-

ganyika. Remarkably, at the outset of this expedition, Stanley had possessed no experience as an explorer or as a leader of men.

Stanley ordered one of his strongest stalwart servants to carry an American flag at the head of the caravan as it descended to Ujiji. After they had proceeded another couple hundred yards, a large crowd of people from the town began to gather around them, and in the midst of the excitement Stanley heard someone on his right say, "Good morning, sir!" Startled, Stanley turned to see a young black man

Henry Morton Stanley found David Livingstone after eight difficult months in which Stanley and the crew accompanying him marched hundreds of miles through the African jungle from Bagamoyo on the east coast to Lake Tanganyika. *(Library of Congress, Prints and Photographs Division [LC-USZ62-78736])*

in a long white shirt. According to his own later account of this episode, Stanley asked,

"Who the mischief are you?"

"I am Susi, the servant of Dr. Livingstone," replied he, smiling.

"What! Dr. Livingstone here?"

"Yes, sir."

"In this village?"

"Yes, sir."

"Are you sure?"

"Sure, sure, sir. Why, I leave him just now."

"Now, you Susi, run, and tell the Doctor I am coming."

"Yes, sir," and off he darted like a madman.

Stanley later wrote in his memoirs that he himself was almost mad with joy following this brief, surprising conversation. After eight months of hardship and uncertainty, against all odds, he had located Livingstone. Stanley recalled: "What would I not have given for a bit of friendly wilderness, where, unseen, I might vent my joy in some mad freak, such as idiotically biting my hand, turning a somersault, or slashing at trees, in order to allay those exciting feelings that were well-nigh uncontrollable. My heart beats fast, but I must not let my face betray my emotions, lest it shall detract from the dignity of a white man appearing under such extraordinary circumstances."

Stanley remained dignified in his bearing as he made his way through the crowds of people until he reached a semicircle of Arabs, before whom stood a lone white man with a grey beard. "As I advanced slowly towards him," Stanley recalled,

I noticed he was pale, looked wearied, wore a bluish cap with a faded gold band round it, had on a red-sleeved waistcoat, and a

Holding a map of Africa in this engraving, David Livingstone began exploring the continent as a missionary in South Africa. *(Library of Congress, Prints and Photographs Division [LC-USZ62-16529])*

pair of grey tweed trousers. I would have run to him, only I was a coward in the presence of such a mob; so I did what cowardice and false pride suggested was the best thing—walked deliberately to him, took off my hat, and said:

"Dr. Livingstone, I presume?"

"Yes," said he, with a kind smile, lifting his cap slightly.

The men replaced their hats and shook hands. Stanley declared: "I thank God, Doctor, I have been permitted to see you." He answered, "I feel thankful that I am here to welcome you."

Livingstone had determined the nationality of this stranger when he saw the American flag. Upon meeting Stanley, however, he might have heard in the man's voice the trace of a

Welsh accent, as Stanley had been born and raised in Wales before moving to the United States as an adolescent. These two children of Great Britain had followed circuitous and entirely different journeys to meet on the shore of Lake Tanganyika in 1871. Their respective journeys say a great deal about the larger forces that drove exploration in the age of empire.

HUMBLE PATHS TO DISCOVERY

David Livingstone was born in Blantyre, in Lanarkshire, Scotland, to a working-class family in 1813. His father was a traveling tea salesman and by no means prosperous in his business. Consequently, he sent his three sons, including David, to work in a cotton mill. David Livingstone worked in the mill from the age of 10 until his early 20s, but he never resigned himself to this grim lot in life. After work each day he attended the company school, where he learned to read and write. He also attended Sunday School, and in his spare time he read books about travel and science. He also read religious pamphlets because his father was a devout Christian who actually disapproved of his son's scientific interests. In 1834 he read a religious pamphlet by a Dutch missionary who appealed for medical missionaries to be sent to China. Livingstone saw this as a way to pursue his interest in science, his own religious devotion, and his desire to escape life in the mill. With charitable assistance, he succeeded in enrolling in the medical school at the Andersonian University, Glasgow. Within two years, while still a medical student, he was accepted for service by the London Missionary Society. He completed his medical studies and was then taken on by the LMS for further instruction with the assistance of a tutor, who described Livingstone as

"worthy but remote from brilliant." Although Livingstone did not possess an exceptional intellect, at least by academic standards, he had other characteristics that were regarded as great virtues in his era. Above all, Livingstone displayed self-discipline and morality, both of which were seen as essential to a person's self-improvement. His early life would be held up as a model for anyone who wished to better himself through hard and honest work.

Livingstone arrived at Cape Town, the capital of the British Cape Colony in South Africa, in 1841. He then proceeded to travel north into the interior, where he was disappointed by the slow progress of missionary work to date. Livingstone soon regarded most other missionaries in South Africa as timid, incompetent, and small-minded, while they came to regard him as rude and overbearing. Livingstone particularly disagreed with many of his fellow missionaries over the spiritual and intellectual potential of Africans. Whereas most missionaries characterized Africans as savage and dim-witted, or, at best, savage and childlike, Livingstone decided that Africans possessed cultures deserving of respect, as well as intelligence capable of development under the guidance of Christian civilization.

One of the reasons that Livingstone began his explorations in South Africa was to create distance between himself and the missionary community. Moreover, he had learned to prefer Africans to Europeans as traveling companions. Unlike most explorers of his era, who ruled their expeditions with an iron fist, Livingstone did not subject his African porters or servants to corporal punishment. This is not to say that he was easy on his followers. Livingstone was not only ambitious but also physically and mentally relentless in his explorations. He would push his expeditions to the breaking point of their endurance, and

Tsetse Fly

The tsetse fly is a small but formidable threat to humans and livestock in tropical Africa. The bloodsucking fly can transmit a parasite, called a trypanosome, that causes a wasting condition in both humans and livestock known commonly as "sleeping sickness." Victims of this disease display fatigue and lethargy, which are commonly followed by death. Explorers in Africa in the 18th century found that European pack animals seldom survived for long in the tropical forests, and that Europeans themselves suffered from lethargy in the course of the many illnesses that claimed so many lives. However, explorers were apt to attribute this lethargy to the tropical climate, or to a familiar disease such as malaria, instead of to the bite of the tsetse fly. Europeans understood that their health was at greater risk in the tropical forests, the home of the tsetse fly, than in the grasslands or on elevated plateaus, but the advantages of open or elevated terrain were again attributed to climate.

By the middle of the 19th century, Livingstone and other explorers were aware that the tsetse fly was a threat to the health of livestock, though they did not yet understand the specific nature of the threat. Later, in 1872, Livingstone was suffering from a case of dysentery that would eventually kill him. When afflicted by dysentery in the past, Livingstone had recovered by drinking cow's milk. Unfortunately, he was not able to obtain milk on this occasion, because the six cows he had brought on this expedition died after they were bitten by tsetse flies.

The threat of trypanosomes to livestock had been established by British scientists in India in the 1880s. Similar findings were then made in South Africa in the 1890s by David Bruce, an Australian surgeon-captain of the British army, who had been ordered to explain why herds of European breeds of cattle were dying. Bruce subsequently proved that the tsetse fly was transferring the parasite from wild buffalo, wildebeest, and bushbuck. In 1901 physicians discovered trypanosomes in the blood of a sick English sailor on the Gambia River, thus establishing that "sleeping sickness" could be transferred from animals to humans.

invariably porters would, indeed, break and run from the column. In the face of desertions and other adversities, Livingstone proved to be both willful and flexible. While his will was a personal strength, he owed his flexibility in large part to the organization and size of his expeditions. From the outset, Livingstone preferred to travel with relatively few porters and servants. An average European exploratory expedition would include well over 100 porters, but Livingstone's porters were always numbered in the dozens, or less. On the one hand, this limited his ability to defend himself against attack. On the other hand, Livingstone was a less conspicuous target without a well-provisioned caravan, and the small numbers of his followers enabled him to move and adapt quickly. It must also be said that the small scale of his expeditions spared him the management of many people—a job for which his personality was unsuited.

Livingstone was, first and foremost, a missionary, and he did not model his expeditions on military campaigns, in contrast to explorers such as Stanley. Livingstone attempted to explore in accordance with Christian principles, and he did so in order to lay the foundation of Christian civilization in Africa. He advocated the dual expansion of commerce and Christianity, which would become the declared goal of all major European explorers in Africa in the last half of the 19th century. Perhaps for these reasons, Livingstone enjoyed the intense loyalty of his closest African followers, even after his death.

Livingstone began his first major exploration from South Africa in 1853 with two objectives. First, he hoped to find a safe and reliable path for Europeans to follow into the center of the continent. Second, he hoped to find on the upper Zambezi River a place that would be suitable for a mission station and, eventually, colonial settlement. Such a place would offer plentiful water and good prospects for agriculture, and it would be free from malaria, the slave trade, and the tsetse fly, which Livingstone knew to be a threat to livestock.

With a small group of servants and porters, Livingstone's travels took him northward to the Zambezi, westward to the coast of Angola, and then eastward, all the way to the mouth of the Zambezi River in May 1856. In surviving the march from Luanda to the mouth of the Zambezi, Livingstone became the first European to cross sub-Saharan Africa. More important, to Livingstone's mind, he had located what he believed to be an ideal location for a mission station and colonial settle-ment on the Batoka Plateau, near the upper Zambezi. He returned to fame and fortune in Great Britain, where he enjoyed an audience with Queen Victoria, received a gold medal from the Royal Geographical Society, and published a best-selling book, *Missionary Travels and Researches in South Africa.* He then returned to Africa in 1858 and led an expedition back up the Zambezi in the mistaken belief that he could reach the Batoka Plateau by boat. The expedition took a turn for the worse when it encountered a series of impassible rapids on the upper river, far short of its destination. The expedition ended in abject failure, but this failure did not ruin Livingstone's reputation as a great explorer. In searching for a new objective worthy of his talents, Livingstone turned next to the greatest geographical mystery of his day: the source of the Nile River. He set out once more from Britain for Africa in 1865, but only his remains would return to a nation in mourning in 1874.

Henry Morton Stanley, like Livingstone, was born in poverty. He was also born to another name. Elizabeth Parry gave birth to the illegitimate boy in Denbigh, Wales, in 1841, and baptized him with the name of his father, John Rowlands. Following a childhood characterized by neglect and physical abuse, Rowlands took work as a deck hand on a ship bound from Liverpool for New Orleans, where he promptly jumped ship upon arrival. In New Orleans he was befriended by a prosperous merchant, Henry Morton Stanley, who gave the grateful Rowlands his name as a token of his affection. After the merchant died in 1861, the 20-year-old Stanley resumed a wayward existence under his new name. He fought for and deserted both the Confederacy and the Union in the U.S. Civil War. Despite this less-than-distinguished military record, the war pointed Stanley toward his vocation as a journalist when he served as a ship's writer for the Union navy. After the war's end, in 1867, Stanley broke into journalism as a "special correspondent" for the *Missouri Democrat,* covering a U.S. government expedition to negotiate treaties with American Indian tribes. The *New York Herald* subsequently hired Stanley to cover a British military expedition in Abyssinia (now Ethiopia), in East Africa. Impressed by Stanley's resourcefulness, the *Herald* next commissioned him to conduct one of the most remarkable publicity stunts in the history of newspapers: the search for Livingstone in central Africa.

STANLEY'S INSPIRATION

Knowing of Livingstone's fame in Great Britain and the United States as a missionary and as an explorer, Stanley had worried that Livingstone might be critical of the commercial motives behind his own expedition—which was, after all, intended to pump up the circulation of an American newspaper. Instead, Livingstone saw in Stanley's arrival his own miraculous salvation. He looked at Stanley's caravan and saw the means to resume his search for the legendary four fountains at the head of the Nile. Livingstone observed of Stanley's caravan: "Bales of goods, baths of tin, huge kettles, cooking-pots, tents, etc., made me think, 'This must be a luxurious traveler, and not one at his wits' end like me." "I am not of a demonstrative turn," Livingstone stated, "but this disinterested kindness . . . so nobly carried into effect by Mr. Stanley, was simply overwhelming. I really do feel extremely grateful, and at the same time I am a little ashamed at not being more worthy of the generosity."

At first glance, Livingstone and Stanley appear to represent contradictory forces in the relationship between exploration and empire. Livingstone, a former medical missionary, was famous for bringing Christianity to Africa, while Stanley was intent upon using Livingstone's great fame as a philanthropist and explorer for profit. Nonetheless, Stanley might have known that Livingstone would embrace the commercial interests that brought him to Africa because Livingstone himself had declared that "Commerce and Christianity" were inextricably linked in the "civilizing mission" of the west in Africa. In the end, Livingstone and Stanley became fast friends. Although Stanley became acquainted with Livingstone's difficult personality, he would return home to describe Livingstone "as near an angel as the nature of living man will allow."

Livingstone recovered his strength within the week, and he gladly joined Stanley in conducting explorations of the northern shores of Lake Tanganyika. To Stanley's dismay, he could not persuade Livingstone to return with him to the coast, as Livingstone was determined to resume his search for the source of the Nile and to complete other explorations that he had planned. Consequently, upon arriving at the coast, Stanley dispatched a large caravan of supplies for Livingstone at Ujiji so that the explorer could continue his work. Stanley then traveled home, preceded by reports of his encounter with Livingstone, which created a sensation in Europe and the United States. Stanley's memoir, *How I Found Livingstone,* became an international bestseller upon its publication in 1872, and his meeting with Livingstone became the stuff of children's books and music hall performances. Stanley found himself transformed from an obscure journalist into an international celebrity, but he was far from satisfied. Stanley was now intent upon joining the ranks of the great explorers and following Livingstone's call to bring "civilization" to Africa.

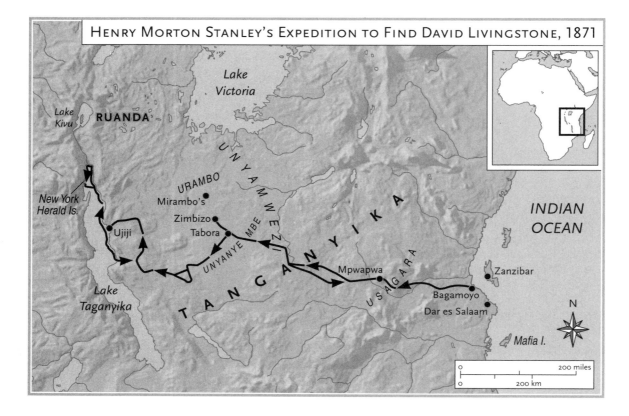

HENRY MORTON STANLEY'S EXPEDITION TO FIND DAVID LIVINGSTONE, 1871

In addition to bringing back news that Livingstone was alive in Africa, Stanley also brought back Livingstone's papers to the British Foreign Office. These papers included his report on the massacre at Nyangwe, which represented the brutality of the ongoing slave trade. This particular report sparked debates and expressions of moral outrage in the British Parliament, providing abolitionists with leverage to push for even stronger measures against the slave trade in Africa. The government understood that most of the slave traffic from East Africa traveled through the island of Zanzibar, which was also a vital point of preparation for all the European exploratory expeditions to the region. Following the controversy stirred by Livingstone's report, the government informed Said Burgash, the sultan of Zanzibar, that if he did not close his slave market, the Royal Navy would bombard his island. In June 1873 the sultan gave in to the British demand, closing one of the oldest and busiest slave markets in Africa.

After Stanley's departure, Livingstone returned to his efforts to find the source of the Nile. He might have followed the rivers that ran north from Lake Victoria and Lake Albert, which had already been proposed as possible sources of the Nile. He had become convinced, however, that the Lualaba River was, in fact, part of the Nile itself. Livingstone's theory, and his determination to prove it, flew in the face of facts that were readily available to him. Most important, Livingstone might have taken measurements that would have demonstrated that the Lualaba River was lower in elevation than the lowest point known on the Nile River. Rivers

Abdullah Susi

Livingstone was accompanied on his final expedition by three able and devoted Africans with whom he had worked and traveled in the past. This group included Abdullah Susi, James Chuma, and Edward Gardner. All these men would depart with Livingstone from the coastal town of Bagamoyo in 1866 and return with his corpse in 1874. Among these men, Susi played a particularly important role in tending to Livingstone during his last illness and in leading Livingstone's servants and porters after the explorer's death. Livingstone had first hired Susi in 1862 to assist in assembling the steamer *Lady Nyasa* during the disastrous Zambezi expedition. Following the expedition, Livingstone had found work for Susi in Bombay, India, where he also placed some of his younger servants in missionary schools. Livingstone then returned to Bombay in 1865 on his way to east Africa and his next major expedition to find the source of the Nile. He hired Susi to accompany him once again, and he came to rely particularly upon Susi and Chuma as he never had before. It was Susi and Chuma who carried the ailing Livingstone on a litter to the village where the explorer would die. Susi was at Livingstone's side in the final days, answering questions, helping him to wind his watch, and preparing medicine. With several of Livingstone's other servants, Susi found Livingstone dead, kneeling beside his bed, on the morning of May 1, 1873.

Livingstone's remaining 60 followers chose Susi to lead them back to the coast. Susi decided to bring Livingstone's remains so that his own people could give them a proper burial in Britain. Remarkably, the other men supported this decision, despite the personal risks they would run in carrying the body back to the coast. Susi ordered Jacob Wainwright to write an inventory of Livingstone's possessions, so that nothing would be overlooked or stolen. Susi and Chuma then preserved Livingstone's remains for transport, after which the entire party set off in what must surely be one of the longest funeral marches on record. After nine months, Susi, Chuma, and about 60 men reached Bagamoyo in February 1874. The senior British officer, Captain W. F. Prideaux, paid Livingstone's followers their wages out of his own pocket and ordered them to return to their homes. Susi regarded this as a dissatisfying conclusion to their ordeal, but he nonetheless gave Livingstone's remains to the British officials, having little choice in the matter. A year later James Young, who had largely financed Livingstone's last expedition, paid for Susi and Chuma to travel to Britain to assist in editing Livingstone's *Last Journals*. Both men would then return to Zanzibar and work as caravan leaders. Susi later accompanied Henry Morton Stanley on his expedition up the Congo River in 1879 and played a central role in laying the foundation for the future Congo Free State.

do not, after all, flow uphill. But Livingstone was not to be deterred as he set out to return to the Lualaba.

It was not the first time that Livingstone made a major blunder in his geographical calculations. This was, after all, the same man who failed to observe the impassible rapids on the Zambezi River—rapids he might have anticipated if he had paid closer attention to his own calculations about the precipitous drop in the river's altitude. The difference here, however, was that other accomplished explorers had presented alternatives to Livingstone's theory about the Lualaba and, moreover, had argued against his theory on the basis of solid evidence. One must wonder whether, for all his selfless missionary work and his lifelong devotion to science, Livingstone the explorer was ultimately blinded by egotism. Livingstone obviously did not respect his most famous competitor in the search for the source of the Nile, Richard Burton, a former officer of the Indian army and an accomplished linguist and adventurer. In fact, Livingstone publicly denounced Burton as "a moral idiot."

David Livingstone died in Africa, and his African followers buried his heart and internal organs at the foot of a tree there. The rest of his remains were returned to Britain and buried in Westminster Abbey in London. *(Library of Congress, Prints and Photographs Division [LC-DIG-ppmsc-08570])*

Although Livingstone's conviction and determination never failed him, his body eventually did. The explorer died of dysentery in a village near a stream called the Lulimala, about three days' walk from the Luapula River, in May 1873. His African followers, under the leadership of Abdullah Susi, agreed that his body should be preserved and returned to his own people, an incredible undertaking that can only be explained by their loyalty to Livingstone. They removed the heart and internal organs from Livingstone's dead body and buried these at the foot of a tree, into which they carved a simple memorial. Although they might have done this for the practical purpose of preserving the corpse for transport, it was an act with powerful symbolism: the explorer's heart buried in the heart of Africa. Livingstone's followers then carried his remains to the coast, meeting along the way an expedition led by Verney Lovett Cameron that was seeking to provide Livingstone with supplies and support. At the coast, British consular officials received the remains and then shipped them to Britain, accompanied by one of Livingstone's servants, Jacob Wainwright, a former missionary student whose passage was paid by the Church Missionary Society. Government officials and dignitaries received Livingstone's remains as those of a national hero, and the former medical missionary was soon buried among kings and queens in a state funeral in Westminster Abbey in London. Stanley, the last white man to have seen Livingstone alive, served as one of the pallbearers in the funeral procession; he helped bear the casket down the central nave of the church, then went on to carry forward Livingstone's work in Africa. Almost a century after Stanley's own death in 1904, he and Livingstone would arguably remain the dominant figures in the modern age of exploration and empire.

2

THE MODERN ERA OF EXPLORATION AND EMPIRE

 Bernal Díaz del Castillo was a foot soldier in the Spanish exploration and conquest of Mexico in the 16th century. In reflecting upon his motives for joining in this risky adventure so far from home, Díaz explained in his memoir that he had desired "to serve God and His Majesty, to give light to those who were in darkness, and to grow rich, as all men desire to do." The light that Díaz desired to bring to Mexico was the word of the Christian God. Díaz believed that this God watched over the Spanish soldiers, the conquistadores, in their explorations and in their many battles with the Aztec and other indigenous peoples of Central America. Díaz shared his motives for exploration with many other Europeans who set out across the seas before and after Christopher Columbus encountered the "New World" in 1492. Above all, the early European explorers believed that God had sanctioned their quest for riches under a divine plan to expand the borders of Christendom.

Exploration was essential to the expansion of and competition between European empires from the 15th to the 20th centuries. The objectives of European explorers changed, however, over this time frame. In order to place the era of exploration that began in the 18th century in historical context, one must look back to the era of exploration and empire that came before it. In the era of Bernal Díaz, European empires were largely identified by religious faith, and they were ruled by kings and queens who sought gold and silver above all else. In the modern era of empire, European empires were largely identified by nationality, and they were increasingly run by elected governments, or at least constitutional monarchs, who sought raw materials and markets for their nations' industries.

A NEW WORLD FOR CHRISTIANS

In the 15th century, the monarchs of western Europe wanted to profit from the spice trade. *Spice* was a general term that European merchants used to identify not only pepper and other edible spices but also silk, gem stones, and other luxury goods that they obtained from Asia. The spice trade had been run overland for centuries along the fabled Silk Roads, such as the trade route between Damascus, in present-day Syria, and Xian, in present-day China. To the considerable envy of the monarchs of Spain, Portugal, France, and England, the Italians were the Europeans who profited most from the spice trade, with merchant centers in Venice and Genoa and banking centers in Florence. In an effort to circumvent these Italian middle men, King Ferdinand and Queen Isabella of Spain employed Christopher Columbus, a ship captain from the Italian port city of Genoa, to find a western sea route to Asia. Columbus instead found the Caribbean, where, on October 12, 1492, he landed on an island that he named San Salvador. Columbus soon realized that he had not reached Asia, but he believed that Asia was not far distant from this and other uncharted islands that he claimed for Spain.

Before Columbus returned to Spain in March 1493, Europeans had believed that they knew of all the lands in the world. They had gathered their knowledge from the classical histories of the Greeks and Romans and from the Bible. Yet none of these texts had mentioned lands to the west of Europe and to the east of Asia, the so-called New World that Columbus and his crew encountered. Moreover, none of the classical or biblical texts had referred to the Arawak people, whom Columbus met on San Salvador, or to any of the other peoples who Europeans would subsequently meet in the vast expanse of the Americas. Europeans were confused by the languages that these people spoke, and they found the American cultures to be entirely unfamiliar. They looked for particular signs of what they regarded as "civilization." They looked for

architecture like their own, but they generally did not find it. They looked for farmlands, with fields ploughed and planted in straight lines, but seldom found these either. They looked for families organized like their own, but they could not perceive bonds of monogamous marriage between men and women. They looked for cities, but most peoples of the Americas did not have large urban centers. This was particularly troubling to Europeans, who regarded the city as central to civilized society. (There were, in fact, some large cities, mainly in Central America.) Above all else, the European explorers were troubled to find that the peoples of this new world knew nothing of Christianity. For all of these reasons, Europeans debated whether these beings were humans at all.

Europeans had earlier experiences with people of foreign cultures, and these experiences influenced their approach to the New World. When Europeans had previously attempted to serve God and grow rich, they had looked southward and eastward, toward North Africa, the Holy Lands, and Asia, where their greatest adversaries were Muslims. Significantly, 1492 was both the year in which Columbus encountered the Americas and in which Ferdinand and Isabella expelled the Moors, as they called Muslims from North Africa, from the Iberian peninsula. The Moors had invaded and occupied much of the Iberian peninsula in the Middle Ages, and the Christian monarchies of Spain and Portugal had been engaged since the eighth century in a religious campaign, the Reconquista, to retake the Iberian peninsula and establish both their sovereignty and the dominion of Christianity. The experience of the Reconquista, and the Spanish triumph in 1492, had great influence upon the subsequent exploration of the New World. First, the Reconquista had established a European culture of

This painting by Jacques Le Moyne demonstrates a European influence on the Timucua's planting of crops. Le Moyne helped found the Huguenot colony at Fort Caroline near the mouth of the St. Johns River in Florida in the mid-16th century, which was later destroyed by the Spanish. *(Library of Congress, Prints and Photographs Division [LC-DIG-ppmsca-02937])*

aggressive, and often violent, religious expansion. For centuries the Christians of Europe had lived under the threat of Muslim invasion, not only from North Africa but also from the region of present-day Turkey to the east. The discovery of the New World presented an opportunity to build upon the triumph of the Reconquista by beating Muslims to the conversion of innumerable heathens who had heard of neither Christianity nor Islam. The experience of the Reconquista had furthermore provided Spain and Portugal with soldiers experienced in the hardships, tactics, and strategies of conquest. The military prowess of men such as Bernal Díaz contri-

buted to the successful exploration of even the most hostile regions of the New World. More important, European commanders also benefited from the advantages of their guns, horses, and their own diseases, which weakened or sometimes decimated the indigenous populations. Díaz's commander, Hernán Cortés, was able to conquer the Aztec Empire with only a few hundred Spanish troops, just as Francisco Pizarro would later conquer the empire of the Incas in present-day Peru. The prospects for conquest and conversion in the New World were immediately apparent to Columbus, who wrote to Ferdinand and Isabella upon his return to Spain in 1493:

. . . Since our Redeemer has given this victory to our most illustrious King and Queen, and to their famous realms, in so great a matter, for this all Christendom ought to feel joyful and make celebrations and give solemn thanks to the Holy Trinity with many solemn prayers for the great exaltation which it will have, in the turning of so many peoples to our holy faith, and afterwards for material benefits, since not only Spain but all Christians will hence have refreshment and profit.

The Catholic Church was ready to support the Spanish monarchy in the exploration of the New World. This was important, because at this time the pope held the authority to distribute any newly found lands under a principle called papal dominion. Although the Spanish monarchy had sponsored Columbus's voyage, it was actually Pope Alexander VI who decided which European monarchy or monarchies would hold sovereignty in the New World. In 1493 the pope issued a formal declaration, called a bull, in which he drew an imaginary line across the map of the known world and "donated" the lands on one side to Spain and the lands on the other side to Portugal. In effect, the pope gave Spain sovereignty over the New World, and he gave Portugal sovereignty over Africa and the lands farther east. The Spanish and Portuguese

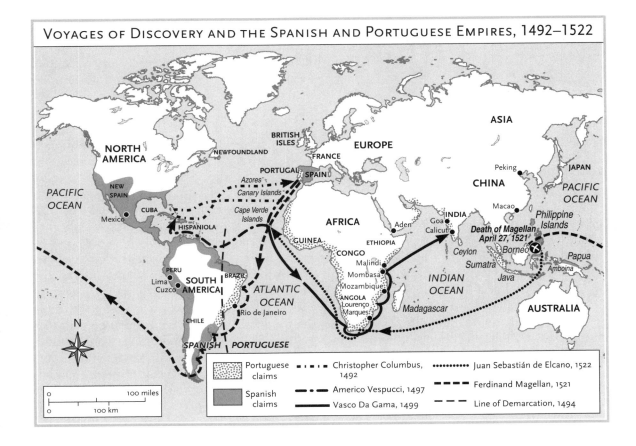

VOYAGES OF DISCOVERY AND THE SPANISH AND PORTUGUESE EMPIRES, 1492–1522

monarchs then confirmed this arrangement under the Treaty of Tordesillas in 1494.

This new era of European overseas exploration was made possible not only by the approval of the pope but also by naval technology and financial networks. The great explorers benefited from relatively recent advances in navigation, such as the calculation of latitude from observation of the sun. They also benefited from advances in cartography, ship design, and shipborne artillery. Access to these new technologies, and financial backing for major voyages, was then made possible by banks and financial networks that had previously supported the spice trade along the Silk Roads. Although Ferdinand and Isabella had attempted to avoid the Italian middle men of the spice trade, they inadvertently enabled Italian financiers to make even more money in overseas shipping to and from the Americas.

TO ASIA AND AROUND THE WORLD

As the conquistadores built a Spanish empire in Central and South America, the European powers continued their race to find a sea route to Asia. In doing so, they circled the globe and established seaborne access to the coasts of Asia, Africa, and the Middle East—coasts from which European explorers would proceed inland in the modern era. Another seaman from Genoa, John Cabot, approached the king of England, Henry VII, and explained that Columbus could not have reached islands off the coast of Asia because the distance to Asia simply had to be farther than Columbus had sailed. Cabot proposed, instead, to sail around the northern coast of the New World. In 1496 the king agreed to support this plan, and he issued Cabot "letters of patent" that authorized him "to discover and find whatsoever

isles, countries, regions or provinces of heathens and infidels, in whatsoever part of the world they be, which before this time were unknown to all Christians." Cabot set sail, with his son Sebastian and 20 crewmen, from the port city of Bristol on the east coast of England in 1497. Following the lead of English fishermen, Cabot sailed beyond Ireland and reached North America, though scholars still debate where precisely he landed. It is likely that he first went ashore on the coast of present-day Maine, then proceeded north to present-day Newfoundland. He explored the rocky coastline and, although he saw signs of habitation, he encountered no people and returned home.

The king's personal interest in this enterprise might be measured by the reception that Cabot received upon his return to Bristol. There were no officials awaiting him, so he rented a horse and road across England to report to the king in person. Henry rewarded Cabot for his trouble and gave him another charter to sail in search of a western passage to Asia. Cabot set out once more in 1498, passed beyond Ireland and was never heard from again. The king would subsequently send Cabot's son, Sebastian, on a voyage to seek the northern passage, but the younger Cabot returned without success. After this attempt, the English Crown would not seriously return to the work of exploration until the reign of Queen Elizabeth, more than 60 years later. Under the queen's orders, Sir Martin Frobisher attempted unsuccessfully to find a northern sea route to Asia in the 1570s, and Sir Francis Drake circumnavigated the globe between 1577 and 1580. It must be said that although Frobisher and Drake were brilliant navigators, they did not make major discoveries. They were more accomplished as privateers, seamen commissioned by the queen to steal gold and silver from Spanish ships returning from the Americas.

John Cabot proved to be only the first of many European explorers to attempt to reach Asia via a northern passage around the New World. King Francis I of France was also intrigued by this prospect and sent Jacques Cartier on an exploratory voyage in 1534. The monarch provided Cartier with two ships and commissioned him "to discover certain islands and lands where it is said that a great quantity of gold, and other precious things, are to be found." In anticipation of Cartier's

possible success, the French monarch successfully persuaded Pope Clement VII to modify Alexander VI's papal bull of 1493. Clement declared in 1533 that his predecessor's bull applied only to lands that had been discovered, not to those that might be discovered in the future.

With the prospect of an overseas French empire before him, Cartier reached what is now Canada. He carefully mapped extensive coastal regions and discovered the Gulf of St.

The Khoikhoi and the San

The Khoikhoi and the San were both indigenous peoples of South Africa. The Khoikhoi lived in clans of about 50 to 100 people, and they supported themselves by herding cattle and fat-tailed sheep. The San also lived in clans, but of only 20 to 30 people, and they supported themselves by hunting and gathering. Both the Khoikhoi and the San were migratory peoples, moving within fixed territories divided between different clan groups. The Khoikhoi were better able to band together and combat the Europeans due to their larger numbers and greater cooperation between clans.

The Khoikhoi and the San first encountered Europeans when the Portuguese commander Bartholomeu Dias landed at Mossel Bay in 1487. The Portuguese, and later other Europeans, were primarily interested in obtaining provisions, and especially cattle, which were the prized possessions of the Khoikhoi. Unfortunately, trading relationships quickly turned violent, due to breakdowns in communication. During one battle in 1510, the Khoikhoi killed the Portuguese viceroy to India as he traveled home. This and other conflicts gave the Khoikhoi a reputation for ferocity among Europeans, and consequently Europeans tried to avoid landing on the cape until the 1590s.

After the Dutch established an outpost at Cape Town in 1652, the Khoikhoi and San found it increasingly difficult to resist European encroachments. The European advance was made possible by superior firepower, the debilitating affect of European diseases on the indigenous people, and the ability of the Europeans to build trading relationships with one clan at the expense of another. In 1658 the Dutch governor at Cape Town authorized a group of company employees, known as free burghers, to travel into the interior and establish farms to grow crops for the supply of passing ships. The descendants of these burghers would continue their expansion into the South African interior well into the 19th century.

Lawrence, all of which he claimed for his king. He also met an Iroquois chief, Donnaconna, and took two of the chief's sons back to the French court in 1534 as guests. These young men learned to speak French, and they accompanied Cartier back to Canada in 1535 as translators. In this second expedition Cartier benefited from the assistance of the Iroquois, who led him to the St. Lawrence River, up which he sailed as far as present-day Montreal. This was Cartier's most important work as an explorer, because the St. Lawrence would become the primary path that French colonists followed into the Canadian interior. After spending a difficult winter on the St. Lawrence, Cartier returned to France, this time accompanied by Donnaconna himself, who unfortunately died before he could return home. Cartier's third voyage was delayed until 1541 by war between France and the Habsburg Empire. After this last, relatively uneventful visit, Cartier returned to France in 1542 and retired comfortably. French exploration would be suspended soon thereafter, due to the ascendancy of an indifferent monarch and major religious wars within the country.

In contrast to the English and the French monarchies, the Portuguese attempted to reach Asia via a southern route around Africa. In the 1430s Prince Henry the Navigator led Portuguese expeditions along the West African coast. Several years before Columbus's momentous journey west, King John II of Portugal commissioned Bartholomeu Dias, a knight of the Portuguese court and a seaman with long experience on the West African coast, to sail around the southern tip of Africa. Dias departed from Lisbon in August 1487 and rounded the southern tip of Africa in February 1488. Dias landed at what is now called Mossel Bay and encountered peoples called the Khoikhoi and the San. He then followed the coast eastward, as far as the Great Fish River, where his crew became fearful of the unknown waters and persuaded him to turn back.

Dias returned to Lisbon after more than 17 months to great acclaim. He informed the king that on his return voyage he had seen a great cape at the bottom of Africa, which the king named the Cape of Good Hope. Dias had demonstrated that it was possible to sail around Africa, but he had also experienced the strong ocean currents that made a complete, round-trip voyage both difficult and dangerous. He would subsequently captain one of three ships in the expedition of Pedro Alvarez Cabral, which departed from Lisbon in 1500 and encountered present-day Brazil for the first time. During the voyage from Brazil to the Cape of Good Hope, the expedition sailed into a terrible storm, and Dias's vessel sank with all aboard.

The next king of Portugal, Manuel, was inspired by Columbus's discoveries to push his captains around the southern tip of Africa and on to Asia. He turned to Vasco da Gama, a nobleman who had previously distinguished himself in naval combat against the French. Da Gama departed from Lisbon with four ships and 170 men in July 1497. The ships rounded the Cape of Good Hope in November, then landed at Mossel Bay, where the Portuguese traded with the Khoikhoi for cattle and other supplies. The expedition next made its way along the east coast of Africa, initially enjoying good relations with the Bantu peoples. After reaching the port of Mozambique in March 1498, however, the Portuguese experienced problems with the Muslim leaders of the port, who despised them as Christians. When they reached the port at Mombasa, in present-day Kenya, the local Muslim ruler attempted unsuccessfully to capture da Gama's ships. Da Gama was relieved to find that the ruler of the next port, at Malinda, was a rival of the ruler at Mombasa and therefore greeted the

Vasco da Gama lost half his crew to scurvy as they sailed back to Portugal from Calicut, to which he returned a few years later to establish a Portuguese colony. In this painting, da Gama stands in the prow of a rowboat being powered by his crew. *(Library of Congress, Prints and Photographs Division [LC-USZC4-2069])*

During his first voyage, Vasco da Gama sailed from Lisbon, Portugal, to Calicut, on the southwest coast of present-day India, and back by rounding the newly named Cape of Good Hope. *(Library of Congress, Prints and Photographs Division [LC-USZC4-2070])*

Portuguese as potential allies. Most important, the ruler of Malinda provided the Portuguese with a pilot who could guide them across the Arabian Sea to Asia. With the assistance of this guide, da Gama landed at Calicut, on the southwest coast of present-day India, in May 1498. The Hindu raja welcomed them, but he would not sign a trade agreement for fear of alienating Muslim traders in the port. Rela-

tions then deteriorated when the raja refused either to receive da Gama's gifts or to trade because da Gama's goods were deemed of poor quality. After open hostilities and hostage taking, da Gama departed with an assurance from the raja that he would trade with the Portuguese in the future, but only if they brought gold, silver, coral, and scarlet cloth.

During his voyage back to Portugal, da Gama lost half his crew to scurvy and experienced other difficulties. He nonetheless reached Lisbon in September 1498 and was richly rewarded for his efforts. The king sent da Gama back to India in 1502 with orders to establish a Portuguese colony at Calicut, which da Gama accomplished with horrific brutality. Da Gama died as the Portuguese viceroy to India, in the city of Cochin, in 1524.

The Spanish king, Charles I (Holy Roman Emperor Charles V), also wanted to profit from the oceanic trade with Asia, but his ships could not travel via the Cape of Good Hope due to the opposition of the Portuguese. Fortunately for Charles, Ferdinand Magellan, one of Portugal's most able seamen, was available for hire. Magellan had been born to a noble Portuguese family in 1480, and he had served in the Portuguese navy for several years in the Atlantic and the Indian Oceans. He had gained valuable experience in navigation and also in combat (he had a pronounced limp, which was the result of a lance wound to his left knee). Despite Magellan's distinguished service, Manuel I, the king of Portugal, dismissed him in 1514, following allegations that Magellan had traded livestock with the Moors. Declaring his innocence, Magellan renounced his allegiance to Portugal and offered his services to Portugal's archrival, Spain.

The Spanish monarch accepted Magellan's offer and commissioned him to find a western sea route to Asia. With five ships and 560 men, Magellan set sail from Spain in September

Scurvy ⤔

Scurvy is a disease that was a particular threat to seamen until the 19th century. It is produced by a deficiency of vitamin C, which results in the breakdown of the protein collagen, which is needed for connective tissue, bones, and healthy gums and teeth. One of the survivors of Magellan's voyage around the world, a man named Pigafetta, wrote a narrative of his experiences that included a description of the effects of scurvy among 30 of Magellan's men. "The gums of both the lower and upper teeth of some of our men swelled," Pigafetta recalled, "so that they could not eat under any circumstances." In addition to rotting gums and loss of teeth, scurvy produced swollen limbs and pain in one's joints. Scurvy afflicted every major overseas expedition until the 18th century, when Captain James Cook succeeded in preventing scurvy among his crew during his second voyage to the Pacific between 1772 and 1775. Although the symptoms of scurvy were well known, it would be centuries before scientists determined the source of the disease.

In the meantime, seamen and physicians combated scurvy by trial and error. They discovered that particular plants could prevent or cure scurvy, but they did not understand the curative properties of these plants. In winter 1535–36, when Cartier's men were dying of scurvy after their ship became frozen in the ice in the St. Lawrence River in Canada, they learned from local American Indians that they could cure themselves by drinking a concoction of boiled bark from a local tree, a white cedar. Cartier's 85 men devoured the tree in a week, and Cartier then brought home other specimens of the tree that were planted in the gardens of the French king. Over a century later, in 1639, John Woodall published a medical manual entitled *The surgeon's mate, or military & domestique surgery,* in which he listed "many excellent remedies" for scurvy. These included "Scurvy-grasse, Horse-Reddish roots, Nasturtia Aquatica, Wormwood, Sorrell, and many other good meanes." He also noted that in the Indies, seamen could obtain lemons, limes, and oranges, which were more effective against scurvy than anything found in England. The superior, curative powers of citrus fruits were later confirmed in tests conducted by James Lind, who published his findings in *A Treatise of the Scurvy* in 1753. The British Royal Navy began in 1795 to provide a daily ration of lime or lemon juice to its men, which is why the British are sometimes called "limeys" to this day. Citrus fruits are rich in vitamin C, which scientists finally isolated and synthesized in 1932.

1519. He took a southern course across the Atlantic and, after three months, reached the bay of what is now Rio de Janeiro in Brazil. Magellan then proceeded south, methodically searching for a sea lane through the continent of South America. In March 1520, as the expedition sailed along the coast of present-day Argentina, the crews of three of the ships became frustrated with their seemingly hopeless search and mutinied. Magellan crushed the mutiny, killing two of his captains and leaving another stranded on the shore. The expedition then proceeded farther south, and in October Magellan's patience and tenacity were rewarded. He found and navigated a passage through high fjords that opened into the Pacific Ocean—a passage now known as the Strait of Magellan.

Magellan confronted terrible odds as he set out across the Pacific. His expedition had been reduced to three ships, due to the wreck of one vessel and the desertion of another. Scurvy was also taking a toll upon his remaining crew. Magellan did not know the breadth of the Pacific Ocean, nor where he could find the nearest landfall. After months of hardship, in 1521 he succeeded in bringing his ships to the island now called Guam, where they were able to take on supplies. The expedition then proceeded to the islands now known as the Philippines, where Magellan was killed in a battle with the people of Mactan Island. The expedition continued, having little choice, and reached Asia in November. A single ship, captained by a Spaniard, Juan Sebastián del Cano (de Elcano), returned to Spain on September 8, 1522, with only 17 crewmen aboard, the last survivors of Magellan's fleet.

THE EFFECTS OF EXPLORATION

European overseas exploration would contribute to significant developments within Europe itself. Spain gathered immense quantities of gold and silver from the New World and established itself as Europe's predominant naval and imperial power in the 16th century. Beyond the wealth and power of monarchies, exploration also exerted influence on European culture and the daily lives of common people. Although explorers and their crews were seldom men of high culture, their findings contributed to the Renaissance, a momentous era of intellectual and artistic achievement in Europe. The Renaissance had benefited from the invention of printing with moveable type in the 1450s, followed by the rapid growth of publishing industries in Italy and France. By 1500, more than 20 million copies of books had been printed with moveable type, demonstrating an unprecedented capacity to spread new information throughout Europe. This new printing technology

While Ferdinand Magellan headed the first expedition to circumnavigate the world, he did not survive the journey. Published in 1886, this engraving depicts Magellan holding a compass and a globe. *(Library of Congress, Prints and Photographs Division [LC-USZ62-92885])*

In 1520, Ferdinand Magellan found and navigated a passage along the tip of South America that connects the Atlantic and Pacific Oceans. Shown here is one of the many existing historical maps of this passage, which was later named the Strait of Magellan. *(Library of Congress, Prints and Photographs Division [LC-USZ62-71977])*

made reports of European explorations widely available to scholars, who in turn addressed these explorations in their own published work. For example, Thomas More, a scholar and influential figure in the English court of Henry VIII, read accounts of the Americas by Spaniards, Portuguese, and Italians. In 1516 he published an important political treatise, *Utopia*, about a fictional, virtuous society that he placed on a fictional island off the coast of the New World. Other scholars, artists, and novelists continued to address the New World in their works. The patronage of these people often had its source in the New World. For example, the Medicis, the ruling family of Florence at the time, were bankers who made great profits through exploration and then used these profits, in part, to patronize some of the most famous artists of the Renaissance.

European exploration also brought new foods to Europe, which was especially important because the European population was increasing dramatically at this time. This was the first significant increase in population since the bubonic plague, known as the Black Death, peaked in 1349 and killed approximately one-third of the people in Europe. Afterward, the European population had remained stable for almost 150 years. In the 16th century, however, it increased by about one-third, from approximately 80 million to 105 million. This population would feed itself in the coming decades with new foods imported from the Americas. The potato, for example, was brought from present-day Peru to Spain in the 1530s. The potato was easily produced and offered high nutritional value; it eventually became a staple in the diet of poor people in Spain and in other European countries, including Ireland.

The European explorers, for all of their skill and courage, brought great and often terrible changes to the peoples whom they encountered in the Americas, Africa, and elsewhere. They had been driven initially by their desire for gold and silver, which they found in great abundance in Central and South America. The Spaniards' desire for gold, and their disregard for the non-Christian peoples who controlled it, prompted them to impose new systems of slavery on the indigenous peoples, forcing them into the mines to pull the gold from the earth for shipment to Europe. In the 16th century, these slave systems would be adapted to plantation economies, particularly for the production of sugar. Due to the large number of deaths in the indigenous communities, and the ability of the indigenous peoples to flee the Europeans, the Portuguese began to import slaves from Africa to Brazil in the 1550s. By the early 17th century, the English and the French copied the Spanish and Portuguese slave systems to grow sugar in the Caribbean and then extended the plantation system into North America, where they grew tobacco, indigo, rice, and cotton.

The Europeans brought not only their desire for gold and silver but also their desire to spread Christianity throughout the world. There were prominent Christian missionaries, such as Bartolomé de Las Casas, who strongly opposed the conquistadores' brutal methods. Las Casas, however, lacked the power to stem the tide of European conquest. Missionaries spread throughout the New World in an effort to convert the indigenous peoples. More often than not, their efforts created serious disruptions within societies, which were fragmented between their traditional religions and the unfamiliar Christian god. Catholicism came to dominate the religious landscape of much of the New World, but the road to this end was filled with conflict.

Finally, the European explorers brought with them new diseases against which the indigenous peoples had little or no immunity. The landmasses of Europe, Asia, and Africa had been separated from the Americas by great continental shifts about 35 million years earlier. The American peoples suffered from diseases such as smallpox and pneumonia, but they had long been free of the broad range of diseases that afflicted Europeans. Both Europeans and African slaves brought with them influenza, yellow fever, bubonic plague, measles, whooping cough, malaria, and many other diseases against which the peoples of the New World had not developed immunities. The most deadly of these diseases was smallpox. When smallpox found its way into a community, it exacted death tolls of 50 percent to 100 percent. Scholars estimate that in the first half century of contact between the Old World and the New World, the latter's indigenous population dropped from about 35 million to 15 million due to deaths caused by disease. These diseases advanced well ahead of the Europeans themselves and weakened the resistance of people who attempted to stop the Europeans' advance. Cortés, for example, benefited greatly from the ravages of European diseases within the Aztec Empire, particularly when he made his assault on the capital city, Tenochtitlán, where smallpox and other diseases had left people dying in the streets. Similarly, on the African continent, European diseases cut a swath through the indigenous populations. Smallpox undermined the ability of the Khoikhoi to resist the expansion of the Dutch, who set up a permanent outpost at Cape Town in 1652. In 1713 a smallpox epidemic almost wiped out the Khoikhoi, making it possible for Dutch settlers to march inland with little opposition. Of course, diseases traveled back to Europe, as well. Some historians believe that European explorers acquired syphilis, a sexually transmitted disease, in the New World, then brought this deadly disease home (however, others dispute this and claim the disease was brought from Europe).

Foods from the Americas were introduced not only to Europe but also to other peoples whom the Europeans encountered. For example, tomatoes and chilis were transplanted in South Asia, where they became regular features of the diet. The Americas also received foods from other places. Apples and olives, among other foods, were exported from Europe to the Americas.

Hernán Cortés conquered the capital of the Aztec Empire, Tenochtitlán, in 1521. His victory was partly a result of the introduction of European diseases into the New World. *(Library of Congress, Prints and Photographs Division [LC-USZ62-99515])*

THE MODERN ERA OF EXPLORATION

Explorers in the modern era of empire—that period from about 1750 to 1950—commonly believed that their goals and methods differed from those of the conquistadores. The earlier era of exploration, centered upon the 15th and 16th centuries, had been defined by remarkable feats of navigation, including the circumnavigation of the globe, and also by the Iberian conquest of the Americas. With great military prowess and brutality, the conquistadores had fought to extend both the sovereignty of their monarchs and the dominion of the Catholic Church—and to amass gold and silver for the enrichment of both their monarchs and themselves. At the same time that they had preached (or forced) conversion to Christianity, they had also enslaved Native American peoples, then imported slaves from Africa when the Native Americans began to die in large numbers. By the mid-18th century, at the outset of the modern era of empire, explorers looked back critically upon the likes of Bernal Díaz and looked forward to serving the presumably benevolent interests of commerce, science, and a distinctive, evangelical form of Christianity. The supposedly kinder nature of this modern form of exploration in the service of empire would later be called into question. In Joseph Conrad's novella *Heart of Darkness,* published in 1899, Charlie Marlow expresses the disillusionment that some Europeans felt in contemplating Europe's expansion. Marlow observes:

> The conquest of the earth, which mostly means the taking it away from those who have a different complexion or slightly flatter noses than ourselves, is not a pretty thing when you look into it too much. What redeems it is the idea only, an idea at the back of it, not a sentimental pretense but an idea; and an unselfish belief in the idea—something that you can set up, and bow down before, and offer a sacrifice to.

The ideas behind exploration after the 18th century were products of their times, and these times were dominated by European empires. There were important shifts in the imperial balance of power and developments in economics, science, religion, and nationalism—all of which combined to change the objectives and methods of exploration since the era of the conquistadores.

THE NEW BALANCE OF IMPERIAL POWER

European overseas exploration in the 15th and 16th centuries had been substantially driven by religion. At the same time that Europeans confronted Islam to the east and a new world of potential converts to the west, Europe itself experienced an era of tremendous religious turmoil, known as the Reformation. The Reformation witnessed challenges to the practices and authority of the Catholic Church from among the ranks of its own theologians. It also witnessed the rise of new Christian denominations, which are now commonly identified as Protestant. The Reformation provoked wars of religion in Europe, culminating in the Thirty Years' War between 1618 and 1648, which proved to be the last major war of religion on the European continent. In the early 18th century, the religious boundaries of Europe finally became stable, and although wars were still fought between European powers, these wars were not fought primarily over religion. In Europe's overseas empires, governments no longer depended on the pope to bestow their sovereignty, and they began to fight primarily over trade. Over the course of

The Seven Years' War

The Seven Years' War was fought in Europe, North America, the Caribbean, and South Asia between 1756 and 1763. The combatants included, on the one hand, Austria, Russia, Saxony, Sweden, and Spain, and, on the other, Prussia, Great Britain, and Hanover. The central source of conflict on the European continent was the rivalry between Austria and Prussia over control of Germany. The conflict overseas resulted from the competition between France and Britain over colonial possessions and trade in North America, the Caribbean, and South Asia. Britain entered the overseas conflict with three significant advantages over the French and, after 1762, the Spanish. It possessed the strongest economy and the most powerful navy in Europe, and its colonial settlers in North America outnumbered those of the French and Spanish, thus providing superior support for its forces. After the British forces suffered an initial, humiliating defeat by the French at Minorca, they proceeded to defeat the French in a series of decisive battles on land and at sea. Most important, the British army won the Battle of Plassey in Bengal in 1757, and the British navy sailed up the St. Lawrence River and defeated the French at Quebec in 1759.

Britain, France, and Spain settled their global conflict under the terms of the Treaty of Paris in 1763. France gave Britain all its territorial possessions in North America and on the Indian subcontinent, as well as some of its islands in the Caribbean. Spain also gave Britain territories in the Caribbean and North America, including its colony in Florida. The war made Britain the predominant imperial power in the world, but at a significant cost. The British national debt almost doubled as a result of the war, and the British government attempted to address this problem by imposing additional taxes on the British colonies in North America. The Stamp Act of 1763, in particular, provoked great resentment among the colonists, who protested against "taxation without representation." This protest would become a rallying cry in the rebellion of the American colonists in the years ahead.

The Seven Years' War had important consequences not only for the imperial balance of power but also for exploration. James Cook had joined the Royal Navy at the outset of the war. His service in the siege of Quebec and his subsequent work in surveying the coastlines of Canada and Newfoundland had brought his formidable skills to the attention of senior naval officers. His commission to lead an exploratory expedition into the Pacific would have been impossible had it not been for the war. Remarkably, future French explorer Louis-Antoine de Bougainville had been among the French forces that Cook besieged at Quebec. One might see the later competition between Bougainville and Cook in the Pacific as an extension of their countries' long-standing rivalry. In fact, France turned to Pacific exploration at this time in search of new colonies and international trade in an attempt to compensate for its losses under the Treaty of Paris.

the 1600s, the imperial powers of Spain and Portugal regularly lost these wars over trade to a combination of the English, the French, and the Dutch, giving way to a major shift in the balance of imperial power.

The demise of Spain and Portugal as dominant imperial powers was caused by a variety of factors. Most important, since the reign of Queen Elizabeth, England had systematically expanded its merchant marine and the Royal Navy. This buildup had enabled the English to fight off an attempted invasion by the Spanish Armada in 1588. It had also enabled Elizabeth's privateers, such as Sir Francis Drake, to intercept Spanish and Portuguese ships attempting to carry gold and silver back to their monarchs.

The British and French began to benefit from their different priorities in exploration and colonial settlement. The Spanish, in particular, had built their imperial power on gold and silver, but this proved to be a mixed blessing in the long run. The overdependence of the Spanish economy on precious metals had limited its growth and diversification. In the long term, the British and French colonial economies, based on both slave plantations and mixed economies of trade and agriculture that relied on family labor, proved to be more resilient than those of Spain and Portugal. Furthermore, the massive influx of gold into Spain had caused inflation, and it had brought Spain into a seemingly endless series of wars with its European adversaries. These wars prompted the British and French rulers, in particular, to build what are called "absolutist" regimes, which were composed of extensive bureaucratic systems that more efficiently supported their militaries. Between their diverse colonial economies and their successful military development, the British and French quadrupled their overseas trade in the 18th century and replaced Spain and Portugal

as Europe's greatest imperial powers. In the middle of the century, Britain established its predominance over France as the victor in the Seven Years' War between 1756 and 1763. The imperial competition between the two powers would not be decisively settled, however, until Britain's victory in the Napoleonic Wars in 1815. In the meantime and thereafter, Britain and France would lead the way in European exploration.

A COMMERCIAL WORLD OF EXPLORATION

After the 18th century, Europe's objectives in international trade and exploration would be transformed by the development of a modern commercial economy. In the 16th century, spices were most often luxury goods destined for the homes of the European elite. In the 18th century, European markets began to expand to meet the demands of what were called the "middling ranks" of society, which developed into what is now known as the "middle class." The middling ranks began to consume more and more goods from overseas, such as tea, sugar, porcelain, and cotton. In response, European merchants placed greater emphasis on these goods, and so, in turn, did explorers. From then on, European explorers would look beyond gold and silver to find other profitable commodities.

The industrialization of the European economy, marked by the rise of factory production and the growth of cities, would also influence the objectives and methods of exploration in the decades ahead. Explorers began to look for the raw materials needed for industrial production, such as cocoa for chocolate candy and rubber for bicycle tires. They also began to look for new overseas markets for European industrial goods. Finally, they benefited from the technologies developed in the era of industrialization. For example, they used steam engines to transport themselves up rivers, and they used factory-produced rifles to defeat the indigenous people who opposed them.

Exploration in the modern age of empire was further influenced by many scientific fields, including botany (the study of plants), biology (the study of bodily processes of living organisms), archaeology (the study of the artifacts and other remains of peoples), and ethnology (the study of human cultures). In the interest of science, Joseph Banks collected plant specimens in Tahiti, Alexander von Humboldt and A. J. A. Bonpland collected animal specimens on the upper Amazon River, and John Lewis Burckhardt located the

ancient city of Petra in Jordan. This accumulation of scientific data was enhanced, perhaps unexpectedly, by the rapid growth of Protestant missionary societies after the late 18th century. Protestant missionaries spread throughout the world, armed not only with Bibles but also the tools of scientific measurement. Missionaries took meticulous notes on foreign customs and beliefs, compiling innumerable ethnographies that remain the basis of much historical anthropology to this day.

The most significant scientific contribution to overseas exploration in the 18th century was the discovery of a method for determining longitude on the open ocean. Longitude is a system of measurement and

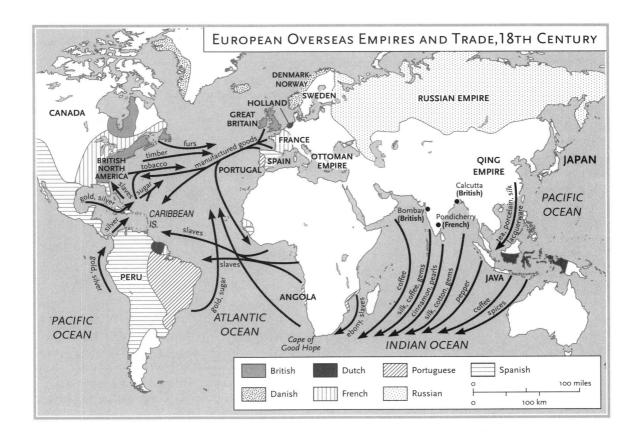

John Lewis Burckhardt located Petra, an ancient city dating back to the fourth century B.C., in present-day Jordan, in 1812. This mid-19th-century lithograph conveys the city's magnificence. *(Library of Congress, Prints and Photographs Division [LC-USZC4-3509])*

location, pictured on maps as vertical lines or meridians, passing between the north and south poles. This system enables people to plot their position on the meridians, in relation to the poles. In the 15th century Europeans had learned how to determine latitude, another system of measurement and location, represented on maps by horizontal lines, which enabled people to determine the distances they traveled to the west or the east. The measurement of latitude enabled Columbus to "sail the parallel," that is, follow the line of latitude, to the Caribbean in 1492. Yet a method for measuring longitude had eluded Europeans, despite rich rewards offered by all of the major imperial powers. The British Parliament also offered a reward, under the terms of the Longitude Act of 1714, anticipating that an astronomer would most likely collect the prize. Instead, a clockmaker named John Harrison devised a system by which seamen could determine longitude if they kept accurate track of the time at their home port or another place of known longitude. The problem was that existing clocks could not keep accurate time on the open ocean because their pendulums and other parts were thrown off by the rocking of a ship, changes in climate, and even subtle changes in barometric pressure and gravity. Consequently, Harrison invented a clock, called a chronometer, that kept accurate time at sea. By the end of the 18th century, for the first time, an increasing number of ships' captains could determine both their latitude and longitude, and thus their precise position on the open ocean.

ENLIGHTENED EXPLORATIONS

The modern era of European exploration began during the Enlightenment. Like the Renaissance before it, the Enlightenment was a period of important intellectual and artistic achievements. Enlightened thinkers employed scientific methods of objective, empirical investigation. They also advocated influential views on social and political relations. Political theorists of the Enlightenment argued that individuals possessed fundamental rights, inherent to all humans in accordance with the natural order created by God. These rights included the rights to freedom from despotism and physical suffering. Political theorists also commonly advocated respect for foreign cultures, even those with different religious beliefs. In contrast to the campaigns of the conquistadores, one such theorist, Denis Diderot, declared that commerce, rather than conquest, should be "the new arm of the moral world."

The changes in the objectives and methods of European exploration were demonstrated in the Pacific, to which Europeans returned in large numbers in the 18th century, almost 250 years after Magellan. The new significance of science and commerce are especially well illustrated by the modern voyages of Frenchman Louis-Antoine de Bougainville and Briton Captain James Cook. Their encounters with Tahiti and the Tahitians also reflected the social and political principles of the Enlightenment.

Bougainville was a French nobleman. He had fought with the French forces during the Seven Years' War at the siege of Quebec, then participated in a brief French colonization of islands off the coast of present-day Argentina, known in English as the Falklands. In 1767 Bougainville was in Rio de Janeiro, Brazil, when he received orders to sail westward around the world in search of possible colonial territories for France, which had lost its empire in North America and Asia to the British in the Seven Years' War. The French government was particularly interested in rumors of a Great Southern Continent somewhere in the Pacific, so they ordered Bougainville to determine whether such a land, in fact, existed.

Bougainville departed from Brazil with two ships, the *Boudeuse* and the *Etoile,* in November 1767, then landed at Tahiti in April 1768. He stayed for two weeks, during which time he discovered that one of his crew, a servant to one of his officers, was a woman disguised as a man. Named Bare, she would become the first woman to circumnavigate the globe. Bougainville proceeded west, looking for the Great Southern Continent, but he was not successful. Instead, he became the first seaman to provide precise locations for the New Hebrides and the Solomon Islands. In July 1768, while anchored at the island of New Britain, Bougainville witnessed a solar eclipse, with important scientific results. The astronomer on board, Véron, was able to use this eclipse to calculate the width of the Pacific Ocean. In September 1768 the expedition reached the Dutch settlement on the Moluccas, or Spice Islands, from which Bougainville smuggled clove and nutmeg plants to the French colony of Mauritius in East Africa for cultivation. He returned to France in March 1769, the first Frenchman to circumnavigate the globe.

While Bougainville's voyage demonstrated both the importance of science and commercial prospects, it also provoked scholarly and political debates in France. Diderot, one of the most prominent French philosophers of the Enlightenment, wrote a treatise entitled *Dialogue between A and B*, in which two fictional characters, A and B, debate the nature of the proper relationship between Europeans and Tahitians. The treatise also contains a fictional story about a conversation between a Tahitian, Orou, and a French chaplain, which A and B also address. This treatise by Diderot not only displays the importance

of natural rights and cultural pluralism in Enlightenment views on exploration; it also criticizes religious biases toward foreign cultures. At one point, A asks B: "Your theory, then, is that morality must be based on man's permanent and unchanging relationships, thus rendering religious law superfluous and requiring civil law to do no more than articulate the law of nature." B responds, "Yes." In the 16th century, a published work of this kind would have been regarded as heresy.

James Cook was born to Scottish farmers and worked as a grocer's assistant before turning to the sea. He received his training as an apprentice and ship's mate for a commercial firm, then joined the Royal Navy at the outset of the Seven Years' War and quickly advanced through the ranks to become a warrant officer. After participating in Britain's victorious siege of the French at Quebec, he was commissioned to survey the eastern coastline of Canada and the coasts of Newfoundland. In 1768 the Royal Society, a distinguished scientific body, cooperated with the Royal Navy to organize an expedition to the Pacific. This expedition had two purposes, one scientific and one secret. First, the expedition was to witness the transit of Venus, which scientists hoped would enable them to calculate the distance of the sun from Earth. The expedition's secret mission, in the wake of Bougainville, was to determine whether there existed a Great Southern Continent. Cook was commissioned to command the expedition, which included a 25-year-old botanist named Joseph Banks. Banks brought a library, trunks full of scientific instruments, and a group of specialists, including artists.

Cook departed aboard the *Endeavour* in August 1768. He sailed around South America, searched unsuccessfully for the Southern Continent, and reached Tahiti in April 1769. He observed in his journal that his men should follow what he regarded as the first rule of trading: "To endeavour by every fair means to cultivate a friendship with the Natives and to treat them with all imaginable humanity." Cook stayed in Tahiti for three months. He witnessed the transit of Venus, explored nearby islands, then proceeded to New Zealand and Australia before returning to England in July 1771.

EVANGELICAL EXPLORATION

Religion was no longer a primary, driving force behind European exploration and imperial expansion after the 18th century, but it remained influential. The religious landscape of Britain and other predominantly Protestant countries had been altered in the late 18th century by a movement called evangelicalism. Before this movement, most Protestants had believed that a select group among them was destined for salvation, and that one's faith was ultimately more important that one's good works in leading a Christian life. The evangelical movement, by contrast, promoted the belief that anyone could achieve salvation by living in accordance with the principles of the Bible, and that good works, in addition to faith, were essential to being a good Christian. The evangelical movement swept through Protestant churches and chapels, and it prompted European Protestants to see the world as a place where their good works might lead even so-called savages to salvation. In response to this change in religious beliefs, Protestant denominations, such as the Baptists, began to establish missionary societies at a remarkable rate after the 1780s. They went out into a world in which Catholic missionaries had long been active. Dominicans such as Las Casas had entered the overseas missionary field with the conquistadores, and Jesuit mis-

sionaries had expanded dramatically since Ignatius Loyola founded their order, the Society of Jesus, in opposition to the Protestant Reformation, in 1540. The competition between Protestants and Catholics would continue among missionaries throughout the modern era of exploration and empire.

The evangelical movement would influence exploration in important ways. First, it generated successful explorers, the most famous of which was Dr. David Livingstone. Second, it became a driving force behind the movement against slavery, which began to organize in Britain in the 1780s and then spread to western Europe and the United States. Britain was the first imperial power to abolish the slave trade, after 1807, and to emancipate slaves, after 1833. Evangelicals, among other abolitionists, as opponents of slavery were known, then recognized that the slave trade in Africa was continuing to feed markets for slaves in other European empires, and in the Middle East and Asia. Consequently, under the influence of evangelicals such as Livingstone, abolition became inextricably linked to the European exploration of Africa by the mid-19th century. For example, the British launched an ill-fated exploratory expedition up the Niger River in the 1840s in order to expose the horrors of the slave trade. In a closely related vein, evangelicals argued that exploration would open up Africa to what they called "legitimate commerce," which would presumably undermine and end the "illegitimate" trade in slaves. In famously advocating the dual progress of "Commerce and Christianity," missionaries combined the influences of modern economic ideas and evangelicalism in exploration. The call for exploration in the interest of commerce and Christianity was taken up by officials and merchants of all the European imperial powers by the end of the 19th century.

EXPLORING FOR THE NATION

Finally, exploration was influenced by the rise of nationalism in Europe. The political phenomenon of nationalism had a number of sources. The most significant among these were the rise of democratic governments after the 18th century, the rising literacy of Europe's people, and the growing influence of the middle class, the primary consumers of imperial goods. In the 16th century, explorers were often not from the same country as the monarch who sent them overseas. So, for example, Columbus, born in the Italian city of Genoa, claimed the New World on behalf of the Spanish king and queen. While Columbus

was celebrated by the European elite, he was in no sense a national hero, as there were yet no national identities to speak of. By contrast, in the 19th century, most explorers had a keen sense of national identity and worked on behalf of governments or businesses of their own nation. News of their achievements spread through the growing newspaper industry to a broader spectrum of society, and the people of their own nation identified with them and basked in their reflected glory. The nation at large, rather than just the political elite, supported exploration to a greater extent than ever before. The middle class promoted exploration by fueling the modern commercial and industrial economy. Both the middle and lower classes contributed

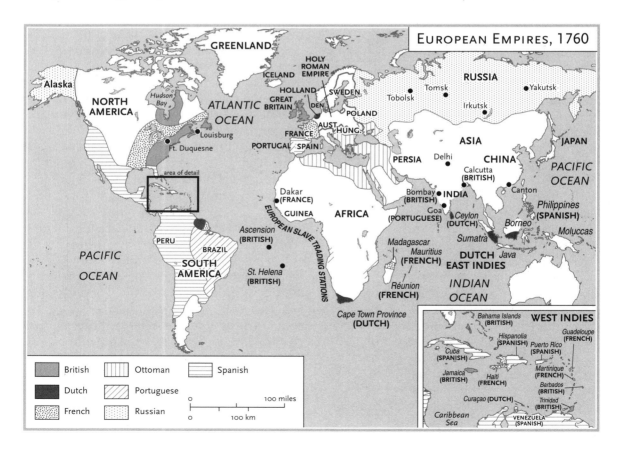

EUROPEAN EMPIRES, 1760

large sums to the exploratory campaigns of missionary societies, particularly in central Africa. The power of exploration in building national pride was so great that it could even prompt nations to embrace foreign-born explorers as their own. Count Pietro di Brazza Savorgnani was an Italian aristocrat who, as a young man, joined the French navy, became a French citizen, and undertook explorations in Africa on behalf his adopted country. The French criticized his Italian accent until he upstaged great explorer Henry Stanley in establishing France's claim to territory on the Congo River. The Italian-born Brazza, the new empire builder, became the toast of Paris and was hailed until his death as a national treasure.

APPROACHES TO SAVAGERY

At the outset of the modern era of empire, explorers were drawn to three regions of the world: Central Asia, Africa, and the Middle East. Explorers sought to advance the strategic interests of their governments and to find raw materials and new markets for European industries. They also sought to spread Christianity, along with commercial development. Finally, and undoubtedly, most explorers also sought adventure.

Europeans pursued many different objectives in their explorations, and they brought with them many different ideas about the foreign peoples who they encountered. There were some, influenced by the ideas of the Enlightenment, who believed that Europeans should respect differences between cultures, build commercial relationships, and learn from other peoples. In Diderot's *Dialogue between A and B,* the Tahitian, Orou, observes: "You would not judge European morals by those of Tahiti, so do not judge Tahitian ones by yours." There were also explorers, influenced by evangelical faith, who firmly believed that they could both respect foreign peoples and improve their lives by changing not only their religious beliefs but also their cultures and economies.

For all the influence of the Enlightenment and evangelicalism, the majority of explorers took a less respectful view on the peoples who they encountered. In 1860 Sir Francis Galton, an English scientist, published *The Art of Travel,* which became a standard reference guide for explorers. He played down the risks of travel, noting with an encouraging tone that young men died in smaller proportions than older men. For those who encountered "natives," Galton advised: "A frank, joking, but determined manner, joined with an air of showing more confidence in the good faith of the natives than you really feel, is the best." He continued:

> If a savage does mischief, look on him as you would on a kicking mule, or a wild animal, whose nature is to be unruly and vicious, and keep your temper quite unruffled. Evade the mischief, if you can: if you cannot, endure it; and do not trouble yourself overmuch about your dignity, or about retaliating on the man, except it be on the grounds of expediency.

Despite Galton's belittling attitude toward "native" peoples, he was nonetheless an explorer of the modern era and not a conquistador. For all of the difficulties that an explorer might encounter with foreign peoples, Galton reminded his reader to bear in mind the common humanity of the "civilized" person and the "savage." "Savages rarely murder newcomers," Galton assured the would-be explorer. "They fear their guns, and have a superstitious awe of the white man's power: They require time to discover that he is not very different to themselves.

3

THE GREAT GAME IN CENTRAL ASIA

Lieutenant Francis Younghusband, a young British officer in the Army of India, dismounted from his camel in the small trading town of Hami, on the western edge of the Gobi Desert in Central Asia. It was July 23, 1887, and Younghusband was on an exploratory journey from Peking in China to India. He had entered the desert on April 26 with a guide, a Mongol assistant, a Chinese personal servant, and eight camels. They had covered 1,200 miles of desert terrain, including 224 miles over just the past week. With what he described as "unspeakable relief," Younghusband now entered Hami, a crossroads for Central and East Asian peoples, including Turks, Kalmaks, Mongols, Chinese, and others. The town was located on the eastern-most border of Turkestan, which had been conquered by the Chinese earlier in the century and incorporated into the Chinese emperor's Celestial Empire. It was not, however, the Chinese Empire that concerned Younghusband, but rather the Russian Empire that was steadily expanding southward toward India,

In his novel *Kim*, Rudyard Kipling examined the rivalry between Britain and Russia in Central Asia, which he called the Great Game. *(Library of Congress, Prints and Photographs Division [LC-USZ62-101366])*

RUSSIAN EXPANSION IN CENTRAL ASIA, 1783–1920

the so-called jewel in Britain's imperial crown. This was the era of the Great Game, a term made popular by Rudyard Kipling in his novel *Kim,* which was set in the midst of the Anglo-Russian rivalry in Central Asia. The game was no friendly contest but an intense, often violent competition for dominance.

The Great Game was played on a vast field bounded roughly by the Caucasus and the Caspian Sea to the west, Russia and Siberia to the north, China to the east, and India to the south. Central Asia is a region of great geographical diversity, distinguished by its combination of numerous deserts and still more numerous mountain ranges. It is crucial to the life of South and East Asia because it is the source of all of Asia's major rivers, and because it is the hub of ancient overland trade routes. In the early 19th century, the area

stretching from the Caspian Sea to Afghanistan was divided between Muslim kingdoms, called *khanates* and *emirates.* Farther east, in the Himalayan mountain range, were the kingdom of Nepal, ruled by a Hindu raja, and the kingdom of Tibet, ruled by a Buddhist monk, the Dalai Lama. The Russian Empire had begun to expand into this region early in the century, provoking concern among British imperial officials in India, who set about fortifying India's northern borders against a Russian advance into Afghanistan, the kingdom of Kashmir, or the kingdoms of Nepal and Tibet. The expansion of the Russian Empire was not fast, but it was steady—like a glacier, as Younghusband observed. In anticipation of the Russian glacier's progress, he arrived in Hami and began looking for a senior officer who was supposed to meet him there.

The officer for whom Younghusband was looking, Colonel Mark Bell, was the director of military intelligence of the Army of India. Bell had enlisted Younghusband to help him in conducting a reconnaissance of Chinese Turkestan in order to evaluate its military defenses against a Russian invasion. Bell was concerned that if the Russians occupied Turkestan they would be poised to invade northern India through the Himalayas. If he and Younghusband found that Chinese Turkestan was not sufficiently fortified, then the British would have to increase their defenses. Bell and Younghusband took separate routes in this intelligence operation. Although they had intended to meet at Hami, their paths never crossed, but they both reached India in the end. Their achievement had not only military, but also exploratory significance, as they became the first Europeans to travel from Peking (Beijing) to India through Central Asia.

In the 19th and 20th centuries, European explorations in Central Asia received far less attention than did those in Africa. Younghusband wrote in 1937, in the preface of a new edition of his book *Heart of the Continent:* "Fifty years ago it was thought that Africa was the only field for what might truly be termed exploration. It was taken for granted that all that was worth knowing about Asia was already known." As Younghusband was aware, this could not have been further from the truth, but he left it to others to measure his travels against those of the great African explorations. "At any rate," he stated of his journey from Peking to India, "I found new ways across the greatest desert in the world and over the highest mountains; and my journey on foot, on camels, and on ponies, was in extent farther than from New York to San Francisco and led across a range twice as high as the Rocky Mountains." Whether such explorations were

equal to those in Africa, they were part and parcel of a greater game of European imperial competition around the world.

COOPERATION AND CONFLICT BETWEEN BRITONS AND RUSSIANS IN ASIA

The British and the Russians had not always been rivals in Central Asia. In the mid-16th century, English merchants attempted to find a northeastern sea route to Asia and landed at the Russian port of Archangel. Finding that they could trade with the Russians, the English established the Muscovy Company in 1555. A member of this company, Anthony Jenkinson, then led an expedition to sail to Archangel and travel overland via Moscow to Asia. He arrived in Moscow in December 1557 and was lavishly entertained by Czar Ivan IV, commonly known as Ivan the Terrible. Ivan approved Jenkinson's expedition through his realm, and he provided the Englishman with letters of introduction to a variety of lesser rulers along the way. The czar also helped to arrange for a ship to carry Jenkinson and his men down the Volga River to the Caspian Sea. There, Jenkinson bought a ship of his own and sailed across the sea to the Mangyshlak peninsula. He then traveled overland with a caravan of 1,000 camels, fighting off thieves, to arrive at the city of Bukhara. This ancient city, now part of the Republic of Uzbekistan, was an important stop along the Silk Roads because it was built on the only oasis in the region. Jenkinson cultivated a good relationship with the ruler of Bukhara, but found that a profitable trade was not possible due to wars that prevented most caravans from converging upon the city. After 10 weeks, he departed and eventually returned to England in 1560.

Ivan IV, or Ivan the Terrible, was crowned czar of all Russia in January 1547 at age 17. Pictured in a lithograph published in an 1883 issue of *Harper's Magazine*, he longed to and eventually did rule a unified Russian Empire. *(Library of Congress, Prints and Photographs Division [LC-USZ62-128730])*

Sir Francis Drake circumnavigated the globe between 1577 and 1580, establishing Britain's seaborne trade with Asia.

The competition between the British and Russian Empires in Central Asia was slow to develop between the 16th and the 19th centuries. Britain had no significant interest in the region for almost two centuries after Drake's great voyage. Britain was far more interested in breaking into the lucrative maritime trade with Southeast Asia, India, and China. Toward this end, a group of London

Sir Francis Drake circumnavigated the globe between 1577 and 1580, thereby becoming the first English captain to complete such a journey. *(Library of Congress, Prints and Photographs Division [LC-USZ62-121191])*

Within a year, Jenkinson was off again, this time to gain access to the trade in spices between the Persian Gulf and India. Again with the czar's support, he traveled via the Caspian Sea to the northernmost province of Persia (now Iran), and from there to the capital, Kasvin. Although Jenkinson succeeded in arranging an audience with Tahmasp, the shah of Persia, the Muslim ruler dismissed him as an unbeliever. Jenkinson was not to be deterred, however, and in the end he established the Muscovy Company's access to spices and silks on the Caspian Sea without the shah's approval. Unfortunately for Jenkinson, all of his hard work was forgotten when

East India Company

The East India Company (EIC) was established in 1600, funded primarily by London merchants. The British Crown gave the company a monopoly on British seaborne trade with Asia and granted the company the privilege of exporting gold and silver to pay for spices. The EIC aimed to break into the seaborne trade that was, at that time, dominated by the Dutch. Initially, the EIC attempted to conduct trade in the Indonesian archipelago, but it could not offer enough bullion to interest the Indonesian rulers and merchants. The EIC then learned that the Indonesians desired fine cotton and silk from India, so the company went to India in order to acquire these goods. It thus entered into a complex, preexisting network of Asian trade extending from India to Indonesia to Japan.

An EIC vessel, the *Hector,* captained by William Hawkins, landed on the west coast of India in 1608. Hawkins quickly realized that his company faced two major obstacles in developing its business in India. First, the region was controlled by the powerful Mughal emperor Jahangir. Second, the Portuguese had already secured trading privileges from Jahangir, and they were prepared to fight to keep the English out. The EIC therefore proceeded to defeat the Portuguese and install an English ambassador at the Mughal court in 1617. Through the mediation of the ambassador, the EIC functioned as a servant of the Mughal emperor until the middle of the 18th century.

With the approval of Jahangir, the EIC built a profitable trade in cotton with Indian merchants. They specialized in calico, a simple and inexpensive cotton cloth. As calico was both affordable and versatile, it became immensely popular in Europe. The company traded primarily in cotton until the late 17th century, when it began to trade in tea. In 1701 it imported about 120,000 pounds of tea to England. Within just 20 years, the company was importing over 1 million pounds. In the early 18th century, on the bases of the trades in cotton and tea, the value of British imports from Asia was comparable to those from the Caribbean and twice those from North America.

The relationship between the EIC and the Mughal emperor would change during the Seven Years' War, when the British defeated the emperor's forces at Plassey and won control over land revenues in Bengal. At this point, the EIC began to transform itself from a trading company into an imperial administration, a transformation that was completed when the British government relieved the company of its commercial interests in 1812. The EIC subsequently entered a period of military expansion, consolidating its control over large parts of northern and western India. This expansion occurred at the same time that the Russian government was extending its control over neighboring regions of Central Asia, provoking an intense imperial competition. Following a major rebellion in 1857, the EIC was abolished and replaced by the government of India, under the direct political control of the British government in London.

merchants pooled their money and founded the East India Company (EIC) in 1600, a company that competed primarily with Dutch, Portuguese, and French merchants. The British government supported the interests of the EIC and waged a number of naval wars against the Dutch, the Portuguese, and the French in the 17th and 18th centuries. By defeating the French in the Seven Years' War of 1756–63, the British became the dominant European imperial power. At the same time, the role of the EIC in India began to change. It seized some of the administrative powers of India's Mughal emperor and became increasingly involved not only in trade but also in tax collection. After the late 18th century, the EIC extended its control on the Asian subcontinent, not just as a commercial firm, but as a government. It was at this point that the British in India began to look northward toward Central Asia.

The Russians made their own approach to Central Asia by land rather than by sea. Before turning to Central Asia, however, they established their dominance over Siberia, the vast region to the north of what would become the Great Game. After the 1580s, under Ivan the Terrible, Russian forces conquered the Tartars of Siberia and succeeded in capturing the Tartar capital at Sibir. By 1595 they reached the Arctic Ocean and by 1639 the Pacific. In the 1640s the Russians began making inroads into Manchuria, which was then part of China's Celestial Empire. Russia's eastward expansion was largely driven by the immensely profitable fur trade, which drew traders and explorers into the forbidding, frozen lands of the far northeast. In the late 17th century, Russians explored the Kamchatka peninsula, from which they saw lands beyond. The question was whether these lands actually connected to the North American continent. In 1725, Czar Peter the Great ordered Captain Vitus Bering, a

Peter the Great ruled Russia from 1696 until his death in 1725. *(Library of Congress, Prints and Photographs Division [LC-USZ62-121999])*

Dane in the Russian navy, to travel northward from Kamchatka to answer this question. During an expedition in 1728, and another in 1741–42, Bering found that there was no land bridge between the continents. He died of scurvy and frostbite after his ship ran aground during the last voyage. In honor of his work, the strait between the Eurasian and North American continents bears his name.

By the early 19th century, Russia had established its power over much of the Eurasian landmass that extended eastward from the Ural Mountains to the Arctic and Pacific Oceans. Meanwhile, Britain had defeated its European rivals in India, and the East India Company was expanding its administrative power. The Russians and the British found themselves moving simultaneously toward

Central Asia from the north and south, respectively, Britain did not want to take on the responsibilities and problems of imperial administration in the region, but the EIC was wary of Russian influence. After all, Central Asia was the source of all of the major rivers of Asia, and it was the meeting ground of Asia's trade networks.

RUSSIAN AND BRITISH EMPIRES IN ASIA, 1822–1914

ARCTIC OCEAN

Bering Sea

St. Petersburg ● ● Arkhangelsk

Moscow ●

S I B E R I A

RUSSIAN EMPIRE

Samara ●

MARITIME PROVINCE 1868

Black Sea

Constantinople ●

1824

1822

Omsk ●

Trans-Siberian R.R.

Tomsk ●

AMUR PROVINCE 1858

Chita ●

MANCHURIA

1846

1854

Irkutsk ●

Baku ●

OTTOMAN EMPIRE

Cairo ●

1873

Tehran ●

Russian Sphere 1907

Baghdad ●

1846 1868

Tashkent ●

1860–65

1895

AFGHANISTAN

PERSIA

OUTER MONGOLIA (Autonomous, 1912, Russian sphere)

SINKIANG

INNER MONGOLIA

Vladivostok 1860

KOREA

JAPANESE EMPIRE

Peking ●

Mecca ●

ARABIA

Red Sea

Persian Sea

British Sphere 1907

BALUCHISTAN 1876

KASHMIR 1846

PUNJAB

Delhi ●

BRITISH INDIA

Calcutta ●

CHINA

TIBET

Yangtze R.

Canton ●

Hong Kong (BRITISH) 1842

Philippine Is.

Aden 1839

BURMA 1852, 1885

ANNAM

FRENCH INDOCHINA

Saigon ●

Ceylon

INDIAN OCEAN

MALAY STATES 1824, 1886

SARAWAK 1888

BRITISH NORTH BORNEO 1888

■ British Empire

▨ Russian Empire

▥ Russian acquisition 1822–1914

N

0   800 miles

0   800 km

British fears were raised when, in the early 19th century, Russian forces advanced southward into the Caucasus, the region west of the Caspian Sea, toward northern Persia. The EIC offered its support to Fath Ali, the shah of Persia, and sent officers on reconnaissance missions into Persia to evaluate the Russian threat, establishing a pattern that Colonel Bell and Lieutenant Younghusband would follow at the end of the century. The British at this time were engaged in a major war with France, a war in which Britain itself had earlier faced a serious threat of invasion. The French were led by Napoleon Bonaparte, one of the most skilled and ambitious military commanders in modern European history. Napoleon's armies defeated both of his major rivals on the continent, Austria and Prussia, in 1805 and 1806. In the following year, he defeated the Russian army in a major battle, leaving France the dominant power in continental Europe. Napoleon and Czar Alexander I negotiated a peace treaty in 1807, when Napoleon suggested to Alexander that they should combine their forces and drive through Central Asia to conquer India. News of this proposed alliance provoked great alarm among British officials not only in London, but also in Calcutta, the capital of British India. The British Empire had not thus far been seriously threatened by the French, but the conflict in Europe rendered the British government unable to provide substantial military assistance to the EIC. Fortunately for the British, Napoleon did not invade India, but rather Russia in June 1812. Napoleon marched 500,000 troops into Russia, where they were soundly defeated several months later, not by Russian firepower, but by the Russian winter.

Britain and Russia allied in order to defeat Napoleon by 1815. With Napoleon out of the way, the Russians completed the conquest of the Caucasus and then looked eastward, beyond the Caspian Sea, to a collection of Muslim khanates, including Khiva and Bukhara. One might say that the Great Game opened with two Russian diplomatic missions to these kingdoms. The first Russian participant in the Great Game was Captain Nikolai Muraviev, who reached Khiva in 1819 disguised as a member of the Turkmen tribe, in the midst of a merchant caravan. Muhammad Rahim, the khan of Khiva, had already warned the Russians to stay away from his kingdom, and he was angered that no one had bothered to kill Muraviev before he reached the capital. Fearing Russian retribution, the khan negotiated an alliance with Muraviev, though he might well have known that the Russians would be back to conquer Khiva almost 50 years later. In 1820 the Russians sent an additional diplomatic mission to Bukhara, with the intention of opening commercial relations. Although the Russians were kept outside the gates of the city, a German member of the mission, a mysterious individual named Eversmann, snuck into the capital in disguise and collected information for three months. Like the khan of Khiva, Haidar, the emir of Bukhara, negotiated with the Russians in fear, perhaps anticipating their eventual return to conquer his kingdom in the 1860s.

The British attempted to counter the Russian advances through alliances with Muslim rulers, and through their own conquests to establish buffer states for the protection of India. The main strategic problem was that Britain's empire in India did not have an obvious geographical borderland to the northwest. In the complex mountain ranges of Kashmir, the British would conduct extensive surveys in an attempt to define borders that they could defend. By comparison, the Himalayan mountain range to the northeast offered the British a clear and defensible boundary, but they soon lost confidence even in this deterrent to Russian expansion. The Russian and British Empires began the 19th century in Central Asia separated by approximately 2,000 miles. By end of the century, they were as close as 20 miles apart. Exploration was essential to the rapid, and potentially volatile, expansion of these empires in the era of the Great Game.

LOOKING FOR THE FINEST HORSES IN THE WORLD

The first of the British explorers in the Great Game was neither a soldier, nor a diplomat, nor even a geographer by training. He was, instead, a distinguished veterinarian named William Moorcroft. Moorcroft brought unusual qualifications and diverse interests to his explorations. He had built a prosperous London practice in veterinary medicine, specializing in the treatment of lame horses. He had a number of publications to his name, including his translation of a French essay entitled, "Experiments in Animal Electricity," and a small book, *Methods of Shoeing Horses.* The East India Company hired Moorcroft in the early years of the 19th century to assist in locating breeding stock for its cavalry. It appears that Moorcroft took an interest in regular company employment after he lost a considerable sum of money in a venture to produce machine-made horseshoes. In 1808 he became the superintendent of the East India Company's stud farm. He was already in his 40s, but he was about to begin an entirely new life.

One might have reasonably expected Moorcroft to begin his travels in Central Asia in search of horses. Instead, he set out in 1812 in search of goats, a sacred lake, and, perhaps, Russians. Moorcroft's diverse interests extended beyond veterinary medicine and

horses to commerce. He was impressed by the Indian shawl industry, which exported fine woolen shawls to Europe at considerable profit. It had occurred to Moorcroft that if one could breed in Britain the goats that provided this fine wool, one could make the same shawls in greater numbers with industrial technology and, thus, make a fortune. Moorcroft found a partner in Hyder Young Hearsey, an Anglo-Indian who occupied himself as a soldier of fortune and the owner of estates in Bareilly, in the northeast of British India. The two men then hired a pundit, an Indian with a knowledge of the languages, cultures, and negotiating techniques that they might encounter in their travels. They were also joined by the pundit's nephew and several porters. Their plan was to cross the central Himalayas and purchase goats, but in the end they would also answer long-standing questions about the river systems of South Asia.

Moorcroft and Hearsey set off for the Niti Pass through the central Himalayas, disguised as Hindu merchant pilgrims on their way to the sacred lake of Manasarowar. They traveled in disguise in order to avoid the Nepalese soldiers, known as Gurkhas, who patrolled the Himalayas for the Gurkha rajas of Nepal, rulers on bad terms with the East India Company and deeply suspicious of European travelers in their realm. The small expedition successfully made it through the pass and arrived on the Tibetan plateau. As they made their way across the plateau, acquiring goats and avoiding Nepalese officials and Gurkhas, Moorcroft mapped the terrain, established the positions of a couple of major lakes, and located the upper reaches of the Indus and Sutlej Rivers. To Hearsey's amusement, Moorcroft was constantly pausing to examine flowers, lizards, rocks, yaks, and anything else that struck him as unfamiliar. He kept voluminous records of his observations, which he deposited in numerous places during the course of his travels. On one occasion, he was surprised by something remarkably familiar: two European dogs, a pug and a terrier. Moorcroft learned that they had been purchased from Russians. He saw these dogs as clear evidence of the Russian threat in the Himalayas, as he conveyed to the Government of India in one of his many reports.

The pilgrims proceeded to Lake Manasarowar, which was and is very difficult to reach at 15,000 feet. This was an important destination in many respects. Not only was the lake sacred to many Asian faiths, it was also widely believed to be the source of the Ganges River in India. Indians and European geographers alike also believed the lake to be the source of the Indus, the Sutlej, and the Tsangpo Rivers. Moorcroft and Hearsey believed that they were the first Europeans to reach the lake, but in fact Jesuit missionaries had been there more than a century before them. Moorcroft walked much of the way around the lake and sent his servants to examine the remaining shores that he could not see. They found no outlets, enabling Moorcroft to conclude that this sacred lake was not, in fact, the source of the Ganges or any of Asia's other major rivers. During this expedition, Moorcroft further concluded that the Ganges did not come from lakes in the Himalayas but was the product of melting snow. The snow of the Himalayas had tremendous power, as Moorcroft and Hearsey found. They traveled through the Dauli Gorge, which a branch of the Ganges had cut into the mountains. The trail on which they walked was merely a scratch on the vertical walls of the gorge, and they watched a number of their sure-footed yaks slip and disappear into the torrent below.

The expedition was traveling in the regions of Kumaon and Garhwal, which were parts of the kingdom of Nepal. When news of Moorcroft and Hearsey reached the Nepalese capital of Kathmandu, the raja promptly dispatched Gurkhas to intercept them. As the expedition made its way home in October, accompanied by a herd of goats and a newly hired goatherd, it was followed by a growing number of Gurkha troops. After a series of confrontations, the Gurkhas finally captured Moorcroft, Hearsey, and their men just 50 miles from the British frontier. Remarkably, Moorcroft was able to smuggle out a letter to his superiors with the goatherd. This letter reached the British government in Calcutta, and the governor-general made a personal appeal to the raja of Nepal for the release of the men. In just 17 days, the men were freed.

Moorcroft's expedition had mixed results. On the one hand, geographers and British officials were delighted to acquire Moorcroft's geographical information about the Himalayas, and particularly its lakes, snowmelts, and rivers. On the other hand, such information would be even harder to come by in the future, because western Tibet was closed to Europeans after Moorcroft and Hearsey's travels. As for the goats with which Moorcroft returned, they were shipped off to Scotland. Many died in the foreign environment, and those that survived produced wool of only average quality.

In 1819, at age 52, Moorcroft undertook his next exploratory expedition to the northwest. This time the superintendent of the stud farm was in search of breeding stock for the cavalry. He had actually wanted to make this trip in 1812, but he had been awaiting crucial information. Having heard that excellent horses from northern Afghanistan might be purchased at Bukhara, Moorcroft had proposed to travel there himself. This would certainly have been no small undertaking, as a mission of this nature required a large amount of

WILLIAM MOORCROFT'S TRAVELS, 1819–1825

supplies, money, gifts, and an armed escort. In preparation for this trip, the EIC had sent Mir Izzat-Allah, a Persian interpreter and secre-tary on the staff of the British official resident in Delhi, to visit Bukhara and take the lay of the land. Izzat-Allah had been delayed in returning, so Moorcroft had undertaken his excursion with Hearsey on something of a lark. Due to changes in the government administration, it would then take Moorcroft several years to get final approval for the expedition to Bukhara.

The EIC sent Moorcroft to buy horses in Bukhara, but, as usual, he had additional interests. Moorcroft remained interested in the commercial prospects of the shawl industry and other money-making ventures. He actually had a rationale for his commercial interests, explaining that a strong position in trade would strengthen the EIC's opposition to Russian encroachments in Central Asia. Toward these ends, Moorcroft assembled a large caravan, consisting of more than eight tons of supplies, which were carried, at one point, by six elephants and forty camels. In contrast to his previous travels in disguise, Moorcroft now looked every bit the British official. He brought his own large tent, complete with carpets, folding chairs, and a mahogany writing desk. His principle Indian translator and negotiator was Izzat-Allah, whose experience on the road to Bukhara proved invaluable.

The expedition initially traveled to Ladakh on the Tibetan Plateau and stayed at the capital city of Leh on the upper Indus River. Moorcroft applied to the Chinese government for permission to proceed into Turkestan, and he waited two years for a reply. In the meantime, he occupied himself with mapping and contributed significantly to the EIC's geographical knowledge of the region. After the Chinese rejected his application to cross into Turkestan, he proceeded to Kashmir in 1822 and closely examined the manufacture of woolen shawls. He then traveled to Kabul in Afghanistan, where he reported that he was being spied on by the Russians. Over these first several years of his travels, Moorcroft acquired a tremendous amount of information, but he did little in the way of purchasing horses. So, in 1824, the EIC attempted to recall him. Moorcroft found excuses to ignore this order from his superiors, and after some five years, in February 1825, he finally arrived in Bukhara.

Much to his dismay, he could not find horses of outstanding quality for sale in Bukhara. Moorcroft did, however, find evidence of growing Russian influence in the kingdom, so he set up a spy network. Over five months he investigated not only Russians but everything from winemaking to intestinal parasites. He was particularly troubled by the conditions of slaves in the city, and he purchased three Russian slaves in order to set them free. When Haidar, the emir, learned of Moorcroft's humane intentions, he forced him to sell the Russians back to their former owner. Moorcroft eventually left Bukhara in frustration, but he would be soon followed by other British officials, such as Lieutenant Alexander Burns, who arrived in Buhkara in 1832 to evaluate the Russian threat from Afghanistan.

The fate of Moorcroft is not certain. From Bukhara he had set out once more to attempt to purchase the horses of Turkestan, which he regarded as "the finest horses in the world." He was told that these horses were with the emir, who was besieging an enemy of his kingdom. When Moorcroft caught up with the emir's army, he found the excellent stallions he had sought for more than five years. The emir initially approved the sale, then suddenly put a stop to it and ordered Moorcroft to depart. Greatly disappointed, Moorcroft set off for home, crossing the desert to the Oxus River in August. His last journal entry reads, "A body of European emigrants would speedily have allies in the natives of the neighboring districts tired of the confusion, oppression and tyranny under which they have long labored."

It is possible that Moorcroft died of fever at Andkhoi in August 1825 while still searching for Turcoman horses. However, 20 years later, two French Catholic priests, Fathers Régis-Evariste Huc and Joseph Gabet, heard word of him upon their arrival in Lhasa. They were interrogated by the Tibetan authorities, who asked about maps. Huc observed in his memoir:

> Maps are feared in this country—extremely feared indeed; especially since the affair of a certain Englishman named Moorcroft who introduced himself into Lha-Ssa, under the pretence of being a cashmerian [i.e., a person from Kashmir]. After a sojourn there of twelve years, he departed; but he was murdered on his way to Ladak.

Tibetan officials apparently found among Moorcroft's belongings various notes about and maps of Lhasa. The priests then met a Kashmiri named Nisan, who claimed that he had arrived as Moorcroft's servant in 1826. Although the circumstances of Moorcroft's death remain a mystery, his many notes, reports, and personal papers were discovered throughout Central Asia in the years to come and provided the British with unprecedented knowledge of the geographies and cultures of the region.

As the British and the Russians gained an increasing appreciation of the importance of exploration in the Great Game, they also found it increasingly difficult to conduct explorations themselves. There were two problems. First, as Europeans, they were easily found by hostile regimes, as in the case of Moorcroft and Hearsey in Nepal. Second, as Europeans, they were easily seen by their European adversaries, who could then keep track of their explorations for their own benefit. Both the British and the Russians

Afghanistan's harsh, mountainous terrain makes passes such as the one reproduced in this lithograph important to travel through the country. *(Library of Congress, Prints and Photographs Division [LC-USZ62-114528])*

solved these problems by learning to rely upon indigenous peoples to conduct explorations for them. The British relied on Indians, and the Russians came to rely especially on Buddhists from Mongolia for access to Tibet.

Tools for Surveying ⌒

The Indian pundits who collected geographical information in the Great Game were trained at the offices of the Survey of India in Dehra Dun. Here they were shown how to use both conventional and unconventional tools of mapping. Surveyors in the 19th century, whether in India or elsewhere, generally used five basic tools. The first tool, used in measuring distance, was a chain of a standard length of 66 feet. Each surveyor also carried a compass, with which he determined the direction of a line. The surveyor then used either or both of two tools, a transit and a theodolite, stabilized by a tripod, in order to measure horizontal and vertical angles. Finally, the surveyor used a level to determine elevations. In the Great Trigonometrical Survey of India, the distances were so great that William Lambton commissioned the production of special, large-scale equipment. He used a steel chain of 100 feet, housed in special 20-foot "coffins" with apparatus to reduce heat expansion. He also built the Great Theodolite, made of brass, glass, and gun metal, weighing more than a thousand pounds. Lambton's men had not only to move the Theodolite from place to place but often to winch it atop specially built "trig towers" for measurements over long distances.

By contrast, the pundits engaged in the Great Game were trained in more discreet methods of gathering information. They were given specially made tools that were much smaller than normal size. These tools were then concealed in boxes with hidden compartments. They also used tools more familiar to explorers than surveyors, but tools that nevertheless provided reliable geographical information. For example, the pundits took "boiling point" readings of altitude with a thermometer, knowing that water boils at different temperatures, depending on one's position above sea level. Given that they could not extend a 66-foot chain to measure distance, they trained themselves to take steps of regular length, and they then kept track of these steps by counting their paces on the Tibetan rosaries that they carried. Perhaps most ingenious of all was their adaptation of the Tibetan prayer wheel for their purposes. The most common prayer wheel is small enough to be held in one's hand. It consists of a cylinder that rotates atop a handle made of copper or silver. Inside the cylinder are scrolls of paper on which is written the most important Tibetan prayer. Translated literally, the prayer means, "Hail! Jewel in the Lotus." Tibetan Buddhists believe that when the cylinder rotates, the prayer ascends to the heavens. The wheel generally has a small chain with a weight attached, in order to accelerate the rotation and multiply the prayers. When the pundits traveled in disguise as Tibetans, they placed their geographical notes in their prayer wheels.

In the 1860s the newly founded government of India began to train Indians as spies to infiltrate Tibet and Chinese Turkestan to gather geographical information. These spies were commonly known as pundits, a term also associated with guides knowledgeable in local culture and geography. The first of these spies was a Muslim named Mohamed-i-Hameed. As a clerk, he had already acquired basic skills in surveying. He traveled under cover to Yarkand in Turkestan and stayed for six months, taking notes on geography and Russian activities in the region. He died of an unknown illness during his return journey, but his notes were recovered and found to be filled with valuable information. Encouraged, the British then recruited two Tibetan-speaking Indians who lived in the Himalayan foothills to undertake intelligence operations in Tibet. These men, Nain Singh and Mani Singh, were brought to Dehra Dun, the center of the Survey of India, where they were trained for two years in surveying. More important still, they were taught how to survey in secrecy. For example, they were trained to take steps of consistent length and to count these steps in order to determine distances.

The two men attempted to travel via Nepal to Tibet, but only one, Nain Singh, reached Lhasa after a year. He succeeded in determining the precise latitude and altitude of the capital for the first time. He also collected general information, and even attended an audience with the Dalai Lama, with whom he drank yak butter tea. He returned to India after one and a half years and produced an entirely new map of Tibet. He subsequently visited the Thok Jalung goldfields of western Tibet, located at an altitude of over 16,000 feet. For his many geographical studies in the service of the Great Game, Nain Singh would win the gold medal of the Royal Geographical Society.

As the British devoted greater resources to training Indians in the arts of surveying and espionage, the Russians still relied primarily upon military officers to conduct their explorations. Certainly, the most successful Russian explorer of Central Asia in the 19th century was Colonel Nikolai Prejevalsky. Over 17 years he led six expeditions, locating many important geographical sites, including the source of the Yellow River. Although Prejevalsky was a military officer, he was also keenly interested in science. His expeditions in Central Asia compiled new information on everything from geology to wild camels, and he brought back many specimens, including hundreds of pressed flowers. In 1867 he preceded Younghusband to Chinese Turkestan, becoming the first European to cross the Gobi Desert, accompanied by a small group of Cossacks. In 1877 he returned to Turkestan and followed the Tarim River to Lake Lob Nor, which had not been seen by a European since Marco Polo in the 13th century. Prejevalsky noted that the so-called lake had become a large, shallow marsh, filled with reeds, due to the decreasing volume of the river in recent decades. From Lob Nor he went south to become the first European to explore the Atyn Dagh Mountains, all the while under the watchful eye of Chinese officials who were distinctly unhappy about his presence in their Celestial Empire.

RACING FOR A FORBIDDEN CITY

The most coveted prize in the Great Game was the capital of Tibet, Lhasa. Ancient Greek historian Herodotus had referred to stories of a people who lived among the Himalayas, but Europeans did not begin to gather reliable information about Tibet and its capital until the 18th century. Lhasa is located at an elevation of 12,000 feet, making it the highest capital in the world. It is surrounded by mountains, and the only means of access are dangerous mountain passes that are closed by snow for much of the year. The environment is one of the most inhospitable in the world, with subzero temperatures, blinding snowfalls, and winds of such force that they can knock a rider off his or her horse. Despite the harsh climate, the people of Tibet developed a rich culture, based on the religion of Buddhism. This religion had developed for more than a thousand years from the teachings of Siddhartha Gautama, who had advocated celibacy, nonviolence, and poverty as means to focus on spiritual truth and thus overcome the selfish desires that, he argued, lead to suffering. Buddhists believe in reincarnation, or the rebirth of the soul, and their ultimate goal is nirvana, or release from reincarnation into eternal tranquility. Buddhists believe there are rare individuals who choose not to take their opportunity to reach nirvana in order to remain on earth to assist others in their own quests for spiritual truth. These men and women are known as bodhisattvas, or "enlightened ones."

When Europeans began to arrive in Tibet after the 18th century, they found the country ruled by a Dalai Lama, a Buddhist monk who held both spiritual and political power. Dalai Lamas projected their authority through more than 2,000 monasteries that were composed of about one of every six Tibetan men. At least one boy from every family was to become a monk, and the monks wielded powerful, and often corrupt, authority. In the era of the Great Game, Tibet was nominally part of the Celestial Empire of China, but Chinese influence in the region had been slipping away for decades. This was due in part to growing competition with European empires that were challenging Chinese supremacy elsewhere in Asia. In reality, the Europeans who explored Tibet traveled within an independent kingdom, a kingdom that had no interest in being subjugated once more by a foreign power.

Franciscan and Jesuit missionaries had reached Lhasa as early as the 15th century, but they had not gathered precise information on its location. The first Europeans to reach Lhasa in the modern era—and then survive to document their visit—were two French Catholic priests, Father Huc and Father Gabet. These priests had been working as missionaries among the Buddhists of Mongolia, and they had hoped that their work in Mongolia would be made easier if they first made converts among the leading Buddhist monks of Tibet and, especially, the Dalai Lama. The priests departed from Mongolia in 1844, approaching Lhasa from the northeast. In Huc's travel memoir, *Recollections of a Journey through Tartary, Tibet and China,* he recounts the many difficulties in their two-week journey with a camel caravan across the deserts of Central Asia, even before they reached the mountains surrounding Lhasa. The climate in this region was bitterly cold, as Huc illustrates by describing the condition of the food that they carried with them, a barley meal called *tsamba.* After breakfast, they would mix the barley meal and tea into a paste and then press this into a few balls that they would carry to eat later. They would place the balls of boiling hot paste in a cloth and put this against the skin of their chests. Over this each man wore a sheepskin vest, a lambskin waistcoat, a fox fur coat, and a woolen robe. "Every day of that fortnight," says Huc, "our *tsamba*-cakes froze; when we took them out they were like solid putty, yet they had to be eaten, at the risk of breaking one's teeth, to avoid perishing of hunger."

In this frozen wasteland, the animals began to die, as did the men. The camels had particular difficulties, because they could not maintain their footing on ice. At times, the

Dalai Lama

In the 16th century, the Mongols invaded Tibet. The Mongolian leader Khutuk-tain Sechen met Sonam Gyatso, the leader of a Buddhist sect known as the Gelug, or "virtuous ones." Subsequently, the Mongolian prince, Altan Khan, converted to Buddhism under the influence of Sonam Gyatso and conferred upon the monk the title Dalai Lama, or "oceanic teacher." It was believed that the Dalai Lama was the reincarnation of the Bodhisattva of Compassion and that he should be succeeded by the next reincarnation. Following the death of each Dalai Lama, his successor was found among the children born thereafter. The prospective Dalai Lama was generally about two or three years of age, and he was identified by a number of signs and actions, including his ability to recognize the possessions of his predecessor. In the mid-17th century, the Mongols gave Losang Gyatso, the fifth Dalai Lama, political control over Tibet, which is why today the Dalai Lama possesses both spiritual and temporal authority. The political power of the Dalai Lama made his position a dangerous one as long as he was a child. The power of the Dalai Lama is exercised by a regent, or care-taker, until the Dalai Lama reaches 18 years of age, and for centuries the Dalai Lamas had a tendency to die of poisoning as adolescents. The present Dalai Lama, Tenzin Gyatso, is the 14th Dalai Lama. He lives in exile due to China's military occupation of Tibet, which began in 1950.

Living in exile because of China's occupation of Tibet, Tenzin Gyatso is the 14th Dalai Lama. Here he speaks in New York City's Central Park on September 21, 2003. *(Jason Szenes/EPA/Landov)*

men had to use knives and axes to cut the ice ahead of the camels, so that their soft feet could take hold. When the camels fell, they commonly refused to get up, and their loads would simply be transferred onto the surviving animals before the caravan moved on. The caravan also left behind a total of 40 men who had been incapacitated by the cold. Huc observes, "When we had all passed by, the crows and the vultures which ceaselessly wheeled above us swooped down on these wretches, who no doubt had enough life left in them to feel the talons that tore them." Father Gabet was nearly killed by the cold, but Father Huc refused to abandon him and tied him to one of their camels. Gabet miraculously recovered as the caravan began its ascent of the mountains, where they lost more animals and men as they crossed icy rivers and made their way through the dangerous passes to Lhasa.

After climbing the final mountain, the caravan began its descent into Lhasa, which Huc describes:

> The sun was just about to set when we had negotiated all the zig-zags of the descent. We came out into a wide valley, and on our right we saw Lhasa, capital of the Buddhist world. A multitude of ancient trees; large white houses, flat-roofed and turreted; countless temples with golden roofs; the Buddha La, with the palace of the Dalai Lama on it: all this we saw, an impressive and majestic city.

The French priests entered Lhasa in January 1846, but their plans to convert Buddhists into Christians never worked out. Instead, they were taken into custody by government officials who questioned them thoroughly before arranging to escort them out of the country. In fact, Fathers Huc and Gabet were lucky not to pay for their visit to Lhasa with their heads. They would not be followed into Lhasa by another European until Francis Younghusband entered the city in 1904. Lhasa became known as a "forbidden city," and it therefore became all the more attractive to European explorers.

Over the next 58 years, the European race for Lhasa included men and women from nine countries. The contestants included missionaries, such as Dutchman Charles Rijnhart, his Canadian wife, Susie, and their 11-month-old son, Charles. They included adventurers, such as Briton Henry Savage Landor, and scientific explorers such as Sven Hedin, a Swede who would become the most successful European explorer in Central Asia in the late 19th and early 20th centuries. Yet none of these Europeans would reach Lhasa. Most were turned back, and some, such as Frenchman Dutreuil de Rhins, died. Rhins was shot in the stomach in a dispute with villagers, who then tied his hands and feet and tossed him into a river to drown.

Even Colonel Prejevalsky, the most successful of all Russian explorers, failed to reach Lhasa on four separate occasions. He made an incursion into northern Tibet in 1872 but was turned back by the winter. He then returned to St. Petersburg and won support for a major expedition to Lhasa from Czar Alexander II, who gave him 10,000 silver rubles. Prejevalsky selected seven Cossacks who were expert marksmen, and he brought 9,000 rounds of ammunition. He also brought a large collection of scientific instruments in order to gather information on everything from astronomy to botany. With an expedition of only 13 men, he proceeded easily through northern Tibet, but then news of his expedition reached Lhasa. Tibetan officials saw this incursion by a Russian officer as the prelude to an invasion, so they prepared themselves to fight. They warned the villages in Prejevalsky's path that anyone who assisted him would be executed.

Prejevalsky was met by a delegation of Tibetan officials just 150 miles from Lhasa. They instructed him to await instructions from the capital, and so Prejevalsky pitched his tents for three weeks. In the end, the Tibetans ordered him to leave the country. Prejevalsky presented a Chinese passport that the czar had obtained for him, but the Tibetan officials declared that they followed only the instructions of their own government. Prejevalsky would never reach Lhasa, though he became the most famous Russian explorer of his era and was promoted to major-general. He later died of typhoid in the Tian Shan Mountains.

The Indian pundit Nain Singh had already infiltrated Lhasa, but at least one more Asian would do so at the turn of the century, before Younghusband's arrival in 1904. This was Ekai Kawaguchi, the abbot of a Buddhist monastery in Japan. Disguised as a Chinese physician, he walked through Tibet with two sheep, attracting little notice. Given that Kawaguchi was a Buddhist, and given that Tibetans were commonly ignorant of the differences between the Chinese and the Japanese, it is not that surprising that he proceeded unnoticed for much of his journey. He was, however, subjected to the usual hardships presented by the Himalayan climate; hardships that were more difficult to bear as a lone traveler. In his book, *Three Years in Tibet,* he recounts his ascent of a mountain called Kon Gyu-I Kangri, which rose over 22,000 feet. As Kawaguchi climbed into the early evening, it began to snow heavily. He tried desperately to find shelter as night fell, knowing of no settlement closer than a day's walk away. As the snow accumulated to a depth of over 12 inches, his two sheep refused to walk any farther. Kawaguchi realized that his escape from the snow was hopeless, so he chose to let fate take its course. He recalls:

> Once in that frame of mind, I took out my night-coverings and wrapped myself up and, protecting my head with a water-proof coat, I sat myself down between my two sheep, with the determination to pass the night in religious meditation.
>
> My poor sheep! They crept close to me and lay there in the snow, emitting occasionally their gentle cry, which I thought had never sounded sadder. Nor had I ever felt so lonely as I did then.

He smeared clove oil over his body in the hope that this would assist him in retaining heat. After midnight, the cold became intense, and he slipped into a state of delirium. "I seemed to be in a trance," he observed, "and vaguely thought that this must be the feeling of a man on the point of death." Miraculously, Kawaguchi awoke the next morning when his sheep rose to shake the snow from their wool. He then managed to stagger to a small camp of yak herders, where he was permitted to sit by the fire and spend the night under the cover of a tent.

Kawaguchi and his two sheep reached Lhasa in March 1901. He remained for 14 months without detection, and he even had an audience with Thubten Gyatso, the 13th Dalai Lama. His reports on Lhasa were revealing, for they undermined the idyllic image of the place as a spiritual center. He chronicled the remarkably severe punishments that were inflicted on Tibetans for even minor offenses. These punishments included blinding, mutilation, and various forms of torture, as well as execution. As a result of this severe regime, Kawaguchi observed, Lhasa was filled with blind and mutilated beggars. He also noted with disgust the stench and diseases that filled the city, entitling one of the chapters in his book, "Metropolis of Filth."

Kawaguchi observed a man named Dorjief, who was suspected to be a Russian spy. Dorjief was, in fact, a subject of the czar, but he was also a Mongol Buddhist from the Buryat region of Siberia. Mongol Buddhists were allowed into Lhasa, and Dorief had arrived as a pilgrim in 1880. Over the next 20 years, he had gained access to the Dalai Lama and become a trusted adviser. Kawaguchi also reported shipments of arms arriving in Tibet from Russia. Within the year, it appeared that his perception of a growing Russo-Tibetan friendship was confirmed. British officials learned that Dorjief led a delegation of Tibetan representatives to St. Petersburg. It is also possible that British officials had no need to await the publication of Kawaguchi's book, as they might have been receiving his information directly. When Kawaguchi left Tibet, he proceeded directly to the Indian city of Darjeeling, where he stayed with Sarat Chandra Das, a spy in the service of the British government of India.

THE GREAT GAME WON

Francis Younghusband had already distinguished himself as an explorer when in 1887 he became one of the first two Europeans to travel from Peking to India. He had crossed the Gobi Desert, following Colonel Prejevalsky before him, and he had conducted important explorations of Turkestan. It is noteworthy that he would then be followed into Turkestan by Swedish explorer Sven Hedin, who thoroughly surveyed the region for the first time. Before reaching India, Younghusband had also become the first European to cross the Himalayas through the Mustagh Pass. Sixteen years later, he was not only a distinguished explorer but also a well-respected and well-

connected member of the government of India. The viceroy, Lord Curzon, had long feared a Russian threat from the Himalayas, and news of Dorief's activities in Lhasa convinced him that India's defense depended on immediate action. He turned to Younghusband to organize and lead an expedition into Tibet to impose Britain's control over the government of the Dalai Lama.

A century before, the British might have thought twice about taking this action, for fear of provoking the Chinese into war. Now, however, the Chinese government had lost all effective control in Tibet, though it maintained a political representative at Lhasa. The Chinese had suffered a major military defeat by Japan in 1894, and the Guangxu Emperor of China was currently confronting a major rebellion at home. Britain had only Russia to fear, but Lord Curzon had decided that the Russian threat was so great that his options were to take action now or never. Under these circumstances, he sent Younghusband into Tibet at the head of a large military column, complete with artillery, in 1904. Despite the superior firepower of the British forces, the Tibetan military opposed them on a couple of occasions with catastrophic results. On one occasion, the British soldiers ceased firing upon Tibetan troops, without orders to do so, because they found the slaughter to be inhumane. Following the collapse of Tibetan resistance, Younghusband led his forces to Lhasa, which he became the first European to enter in almost 60 years. He found neither the Dalai Lama, who had fled into a temporary exile, nor evidence of Russian influence. In September 1904 he signed the Anglo-Tibetan Convention with the Dalai Lama's regent, who had remained behind with the Dalai Lama's official seal. This convention opened Tibet to British commerce, prevented the Tibetans from dealing with other powers

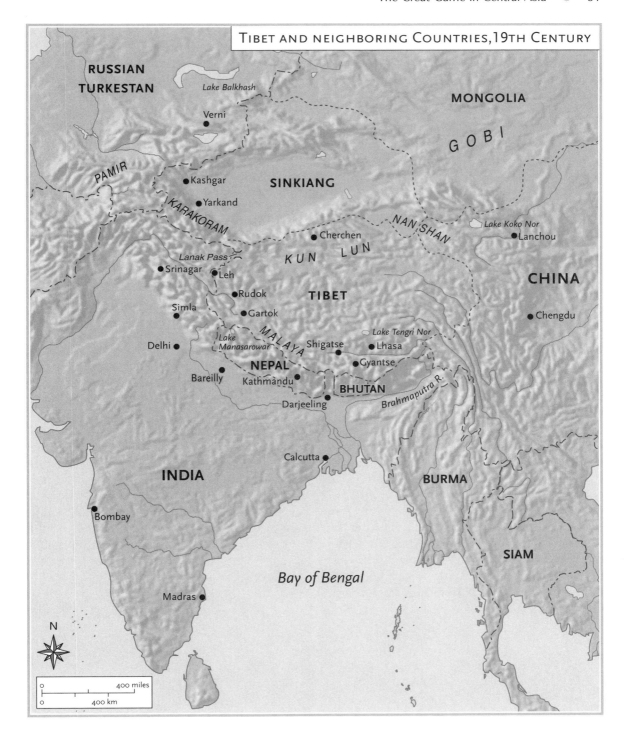

TIBET AND NEIGHBORING COUNTRIES, 19TH CENTURY

RUSSIAN TURKESTAN

Lake Balkhash

Verni

MONGOLIA

GOBI

PAMIR

KARAKORAM

Kashgar

Yarkand

SINKIANG

NAN SHAN

Lake Koko Nor

Lanchou

Cherchen

KUN LUN

CHINA

Lanak Pass

Srinagar

Leh

Rudok

Gartok

TIBET

Chengdu

Simla

MALAYA

Lake Manasarowar

Shigatse

Lake Tengri Nor

Lhasa

Delhi

NEPAL

Gyantse

Bareilly

Kathmandu

BHUTAN

Brahmaputra R.

Darjeeling

Calcutta

INDIA

BURMA

Bombay

Bay of Bengal

SIAM

Madras

N

0   400 miles

0   400 km

without British approval, and provided for a British occupation force until the Tibetan government paid the cost of Younghusband's expedition.

So the British claimed the most coveted prize in the Great Game, but the game was actually concluded by developments outside Central Asia. Most important, after the late 19th century, Germany became a dangerous rival of both Britain and Russia, pushing the two nations into an uneasy alliance. Also, within 13 years of the Anglo-Tibetan Convention, the czarist regime in Russia was overthrown and replaced by a revolutionary government that had more immediate concerns than boundary lines in Central Asia. But even after the Great Game, important explorations in Central Asia would continue. Again Younghusband was followed by Hedin, who, in the years after the Anglo-Tibetan Convention, traveled throughout southern Tibet and compiled a nine-volume, comprehensive geographical survey, accompanied by three volumes of maps. And Younghusband's own work was far from finished. He would subsequently return to the Himalayas and support the exploration of the top of the world, the peak of Mount Everest.

Imperial rivalries had driven European explorations in Central Asia over the course of the 19th century, and these explorations had been followed from Bukhara to Lhasa by the assertion of Europe's political dominance. The influence of European imperial administrations did not, however, change the daily lives of the many peoples of Central Asia to a great

extent before the outbreak of World War I in 1914. European Christian missionaries were greatly discouraged by their failure to win mass conversions among the Muslims, Buddhists, and Hindus of the region. Likewise, European commerce was slow to expand in Central Asia, and the region remained largely untouched by industrial development for many decades. There were Russians who attempted to establish colonial settlements in Central Asia, but the harsh climate and unforgiving terrain most often sent them home. As the British were primarily concerned with the defense of India, their own incursions into Central Asia were limited to military expeditions. Having no desire to assume additional administrative responsibilities, the British were content to respect the political autonomy of Tibet and Nepal, even after the heavy-handed Anglo-Tibetan Convention of 1904. As Europeans continued their explorations well into the 1920s and 1930s, they commonly met people who had never seen a watch, a magnifying glass, or a breech-loading rifle. These people went about their lives much as their great-grandparents had done, unaware of the many scientific and technological developments that had transformed society in the West over the previous two centuries. This situation would begin to change throughout much of Central Asia only after the 1930s and 1940s, when the communist regimes of the Soviet Union and China imposed comprehensive programs of industrial development and economic and social reform.

4

FOLLOWING THE NIGER
AND THE NILE

The modern era of the European exploration of the great rivers of Africa began in a London tavern. In June 1788, Sir Joseph Banks, formerly the chief scientist on Captain Cook's first expedition to the Pacific and now the president of the Royal Society, was having dinner with 11 influential friends. These 12 men shared many interests in science, and especially geography, which they were prepared to advance with their own considerable wealth. They accordingly drafted and passed the following resolution:

> That, as no species of information is more ardently desired, or more generally useful, than that which improves the science of Geography; and as the vast Continent of Africa, notwithstanding the efforts of the Ancients, and the wishes of the Moderns, is still in a great measure unexplored, the members of this Club do form themselves into an Association for Promoting the Discovery of the Inland Parts of that Quarter of the world.

The 12 men thus founded the Association for Promoting the Discovery of the Interior Parts of Africa. Recognizing that rivers provided a ready means of traveling into the African interior, they chose the exploration of the Niger River as their first object. Although Europeans understood that the Niger played a vital role in the life of West Africa, they did not know where the river ended. By contrast, the mystery of the Nile River in the northeast of Africa lay not in its end, but in its beginning. In the years after Europeans resolved the mystery of the Niger, the Association for Promoting the Discovery of the Interior Parts of Africa was absorbed into the Geographical Society of London in 1831. This organization would be renamed the Royal Geographical Society and pursue the discovery of the source of the Nile as the greatest geographical cause of the 19th century.

Europeans had a variety of motives for attempting to track these two great rivers. The members of Banks's dinner club wanted to extend scientific knowledge and to evaluate commercial prospects in the African interior. Others desired to expose and combat the African slave trade or to spread the Christian faith. The last two objectives became all the more important after the British government abolished the slave trade in 1807 and then emancipated slaves in the British Empire after 1833. Explorers of all kinds, and especially missionaries, subsequently described their expeditions as means to expose and stop slavery in Africa. They intended to replace the slave trade with what they called "legitimate commerce" between Africans and Europeans. This commerce would include raw materials necessary to European industries and the products of those industries exported to the African market. In addition to industrial commerce in items ranging from palm oil to calico, Europeans also sought ivory from the tusks of elephants, which they transformed into everything from combs to piano keys. The combination of commerce and Christianity as driving forces in European exploration threatened many African rulers, and particularly those of North and East Africa. The economies of these regions relied heavily upon slavery, and the societies were predominantly Muslim. Given that European explorers commonly approached the Niger and Nile Rivers from the north and the east, their commitments to abolition and their Christian faith created obstacles to their progress as great as the terrain and environment of Africa itself.

FINDING THE NIGER

The Niger River flows for 2,600 miles, making it one of the longest rivers in the world. It is the only major river in Africa that begins by flowing away from the ocean, which is just one reason why European explorers and geographers had so much trouble in determining its course. The river begins 150 miles from the West African coast, in the Futa Jalon uplands between present-day Guinea and Sierra Leone. It then flows northeastward to the southern edge of the Sahara Desert, where it turns southeast to empty, over a thousand miles beyond, through hundreds of creeks into the Gulf of Guinea. In addition to the unusual starting point of the Niger, several other factors made the river difficult for Europeans to find. The Sahara Desert to the north was a formidable obstacle, as was the hostility of many Muslims in the region to exploration by Christians. While desolate terrain, terrible heat, and the animosity of Muslims complicated the northern approach to the river, the West African coast harbored diseases that killed Europeans at alarming rates, prompting Europeans to refer to the region as the "white man's grave." Finally, the mouth of the Niger is not obvious, because it takes the form of a delta with numerous outlets to the ocean. It had been much easier, by contrast, for Europeans to locate the mouth of the Congo River, which turns the Atlantic a muddy brown for miles offshore. For more than 2,000 years Europeans had wondered about the course of the Niger and where it met the sea. The ancient historian Herodotus acknowledged the existence of the river, but he did not attempt to locate it. Others speculated that it might travel beneath the Sahara Desert and empty into the Mediterranean. Still others argued that it emptied into a salt lake in the middle of Africa or that it flowed into the Nile to the northeast.

In the late 18th century, European geographers generally regarded Leo Africanus as their best authority on the possible course of the Niger. Africanus is the name most commonly given to a Muslim from Spain who moved to North Africa after the Christian monarchs Ferdinand and Isabella reconquered the Iberian Peninsula in 1492. As a young man, he was later captured at sea by Christians and, through a series of remarkable circumstances, introduced to Pope Leo X. He converted to Christianity and was baptized Giovanni Leone. At the pope's suggestion, he learned Italian and published an account of his travels and experiences in Africa, which was then translated into English in 1600 under the title *History and Description of Africa and the Notable Things Contained Therein*. There were two parts of this description that had lasting influence on European views of the Niger River, in particular. First, Africanus reported that the Niger flows westward to the sea. Second, he said that the city of Timbuktu, just north of the river in the southern Sahara, was a place of extraordinary wealth. Timbuktu was located on an ancient caravan route and had long been a major market for traders from both North and West Africa. According to Africanus, Timbuktu was ruled by a king who ate off plates of gold and possessed many gold scepters, some of which weighed 1,300 pounds. By the late 18th century, Timbuktu had become a legend in Europe: a city of gold in the desert sands.

With virtually no hard and accurate information at hand, the Association for Promoting the Discovery of the Interior Parts of Africa decided that it should approach the Niger from the northeast, setting out from Egypt. The initial attempt was not, however, promising. The association's first explorer, an American named John Ledyard, reached Cairo and then died of a "bilious complaint." The second explorer, an Englishman named Simon Lucas, traveled as far as southern Libya before he turned back. Following Ledyard's failed expedition, the association had begun preparing to approach the Niger from the west. Its third explorer was Daniel Houghton, an Irishman, who landed on the coast of the Gambia and then traveled inland on horseback. Although he made it into the interior, he was robbed and murdered by Muslim merchants.

With this string of failures behind him, Joseph Banks turned to a young acquaintance of his, Mungo Park, a Scottish doctor with an

During his first exploration of Africa, Mungo Park learned that the Niger River flowed eastward. He and his party explored the Niger River to a greater extent on his second journey but were killed within 600 miles of its mouth. *(Library of Congress, Prints and Photographs Division [LC-USZ62-78115])*

interest in botany who had recently served as a ship's surgeon. In 1796 the association instructed Park to follow Houghton's path to the Niger. Park accordingly landed on the Gambian coast and then pointed his horse in a northeasterly direction. Traveling through the lands of the Mandingo, Foulah, and Bambarran, he underwent numerous hardships, including fever, robbery, and imprisonment. Finally, he had the good fortune to join a caravan of Kaartans, members of a tribe who were fleeing local wars. The Kaartans brought him to the Niger and then to Segu, the capital of Bambarra. Contrary to the expectation of Banks and his other employers, Park found that the Niger flowed *eastward,* which actually did not surprise him, for he had been told by many Africans along the way that the river flowed toward the rising sun. Park arrived on the Niger empty-handed, hungry, and fatigued, so he turned to the king of Segu, Mansong, for assistance. When Park attempted to get passage across the river to the king's home, he was stopped by the king's representatives, who ordered him to wait at a nearby village. As Park later discerned, the king was worried that if he received this Christian traveler, he might offend his Muslim subjects.

Park arrived at the village only to discover that no one would give him shelter. He sat beneath a tree, hungry and dejected, dreading the prospect of sleeping outside in the rain. In his book, *Travels in the Interior Districts of Africa,* Park recalled:

> I was regarded with astonishment and fear, and was obliged to sit all day without victuals, in the shade of a tree; and the night threatened to be very uncomfortable, for the wind rose, and there was great appearance of a heavy rain; and the wild beasts are so very numerous in the neighborhood, that I should have been under the necessity of climbing up the tree, and resting among the branches.

At this point, like so many European explorers before and after him, Park benefited from the charity of an African woman. She saw him as she returned from working in the fields and paused to talk. ". . . With looks of great compassion," Park observed, "she took up my saddle and bridle, and told me to follow her. Having conducted me into her hut, she lighted up a lamp, spread a mat on the floor, and told me I might remain there for the night." The woman fed Park, who then fell asleep as she and other women of the household spun cotton thread and sang about him. "The winds roared, the rains fell.—The poor white man, faint and weary, came and sat under our tree.—He has no mother to bring him milk; no wife to grind his corn." In a chorus, the women sang, "Let us pity the white man; no mother has he . . ." Park, who understood their language, was overwhelmed by this kindness. When he departed in the morning, he gave the woman two of the four remaining brass buttons from his waistcoat.

King Mansong refused to receive Park. Instead, he sent Park a bag of 5,000 cowrie shells—a large sum of the regional currency—and provided a guide to lead him away from Segu. Park chose to continue eastward to Silla, where he finally decided to turn back. Before traveling west, however, he attempted to learn all that he could about the lands downriver. He learned that he was a week short of Timbuktu and about two weeks' journey from the kingdom of Houssa, the capital of which was supposedly larger and more prosperous than Timbuktu. "Of the further progress of this great river, and its final exit," Park explained, "all the natives with whom I conversed, seem to be entirely ignorant." The people of Silla were aware of people who traveled up river from the east to trade at Houssa and Timbuktu, but these people spoke unfamiliar languages. Even those eastern traders who spoke Arabic could only describe the length of the river in general terms. According to Park, "They believe *it runs to the world's end.*"

Park turned westward in August and traveled through heavy rains. His journal of August 5 stated, "I departed from Nyamee; but the country was so deluged that I was frequently in danger of losing the road, and had to wade across the savannahs for miles together, knee deep in water. Even the corn ground, which is the driest land in the country, was so completely flooded, that my horse twice stuck fast in the mud, and was not got out without the greatest difficulty." After leaving the river, Park was again robbed, this time by a band of Foulah men. They stripped him naked and took everything, including his horse and compass. Before they left, they tossed him a shirt, his trousers, and his hat—the most important of his possessions, because it contained his many notes stuck inside the crown. "After they were gone," Park recalls, "I sat for some time, looking around me with amazement and terror . . . I saw myself in the midst of a vast wilderness, in the depth of the rainy season; naked and alone; surrounded by savage animals, and men still more savage. I was five hundred miles from the nearest European settlement."

Park made his way to the town of Sibidooloo, a frontier settlement of the kingdom of Manding. To Park's great surprise, the chief received him with kindness and assured him that he would retrieve his belongings. To Park's still greater surprise, his belongings were in fact returned, enabling him to continue his journey in early September. Like many European explorers after him, Park joined a slave caravan for both protection and guidance to the coast. He struck up a friendship with

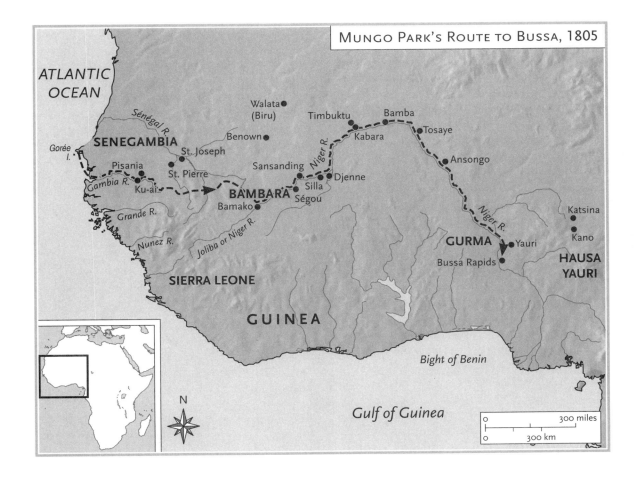

the slave trader named Karfa, who was with Park when he was joyfully met by English merchants who regarded him as one returned from the dead. After arranging for one of the merchants to pay Karfa the value of two fine slaves, Park caught a slave ship to Antigua in the Caribbean, from which he then returned to Britain. His report that the Niger flows eastward, rather than westward, settled a major issue of African geography. Park became famous, and his book, *Travels in the Interior Districts of Africa*, sold out the first 1,500 copies in one week.

The British government sent Park back to the Niger in 1805 to follow the river to its end. In contrast to Banks's association of armchair geographers, whose interests were largely scientific, the Colonial Office was exclusively interested in trade. This time, with commercial interests at stake, Park was supported by a large expedition. He collected 40 British troops from a garrison on Goree Island, off the coast of Gambia, and then sailed up the river in April to Kayee. He then marched his expedition overland toward the Niger, but his men were decimated by fever and dysentery. In June men were dying so often that Park no longer stopped to bury them, nor did he wait for the sick who could no longer keep up with the column. He had to conserve the remaining energy of his surviving followers, particularly as they now carried their own supplies, because all of the pack animals had died. The remnants of the column reached the Niger on August 19, and Park returned to the same King Mansong who had previously given him 5,000 cowrie shells to go away. The king was once more eager to rid himself of Park, so he helped Park build a vessel on which to sail down the Niger in November. Perhaps recalling his previous difficulties with thieves and local chiefs, Park took onboard as many supplies as possible in order to avoid having to stop again on

shore. His strategy was simple: Keep moving and shoot any one who approached. Apparently, it did not work. Although the precise circumstances of the deaths of Park and his men remain mysterious, it appears probable that the expedition ended in an ambush on the Bussa Rapids, just 600 miles from the mouth of the river. Not long before his death, Park had allowed one of his guides to return west and given this man letters and notes to send to London. Consequently, later explorers knew a great deal more about the Niger River and were left with only one question: Where did it end?

Hugh Clapperton died leading an expedition to Africa on behalf of Britain. *(Library of Congress, Prints and Photographs Division [LC-USZ62-78116])*

The British government sponsored two more failed expeditions to explore the Niger. On the second of these expeditions, the leader, Hugh Clapperton, was accompanied by a servant named Richard Lander, the uneducated son of a Cornish farmer. Clapperton died, but Lander survived to return home. The British government then offered to send Lander back to West Africa in 1830 with his younger brother, John. The Landers had no scientific or commercial expertise to bring to West Africa, but the government was short of volunteers to travel to the "white man's grave," as it was known, and the Landers were prepared to work for little money. On the bases of both Park's notes and speculations by geographers, the Landers decided to begin their march to the Niger at Badagri, on the Bight of Benin. Their plan was to locate the Niger several hundred miles from the coast, and then follow it to its end, which would turn out to be just 200 miles southeast

Malaria and Quinine

Malaria is a disease caused by a blood parasite passed on to humans by the bite of certain kinds of mosquitoes. Accounts of malaria appear in the classical texts of the Greeks and Romans, and it has been present in most tropical and temperate parts of the world at one time or another. In the 18th and 19th centuries, Europeans generally referred to malaria as "fever." The symptoms ranged from debilitating weakness and aching limbs to intense headaches, loss of appetite, and delirium. Malaria can result in death, as it commonly did among Europeans in Africa until the mid-19th century.

Although almost all European explorers in Africa endured bouts of fever, few could agree on its cause. The most common explanation was that "miasmas" from swamps produced fever. Some believed that it was caused by strenuous activity in damp clothing, while others believed that it was carried in rain. David Livingstone was the only major explorer to propose that fever was somehow caused by mosquitoes. Given the variety of possible causes of fever, there were many possible cures, virtually all of which did not work. Some doctors recommended a cold bath, while others recommended swallowing arsenic. In fact, Europeans had been aware of an effective cure for fever since the 16th century, when the indigenous peoples of Peru informed Jesuit missionaries that fever could be cured by drinking an infusion made with the bark of the Cinchona tree. Still, no one understood what it was about the bark that made it effective in combating fever. In the 19th century, two French pharmacists answered this question by isolating the curative agent in the bark, which is called quinine. It became possible after 1820 to obtain quinine powder to be taken in prescribed dosages. Quinine became widely available in the 1850s, when the Dutch began to cultivate the bark in Java. It is no exaggeration to say that the mass production and distribution of quinine made possible the subsequent European "scramble for Africa."

of Badagri. The plan worked very well over the course of a few months. The Landers reached the Niger near Bussa, then they acquired canoes and sailed down the river, observing the Benue River as it ran into the Niger about 250 miles from the coast. Before reaching the coast, however, they were taken prisoner by Ibo pirates and presented to the Ibo king. The king sold the Landers to his son-in-law, who then took them to the coast to be ransomed to a European vessel. As the Landers were carried down the river to an uncertain fate, they saw seagulls and evidence of ocean tides, confirming that they had succeeded in their exploratory mission. Whether they would survive their imprisonment and report their findings was another matter. It appeared fortunate, at first, that when they reached the coast there was a vessel at anchor from Liverpool, England. But to the Landors' dismay, the captain initially refused to pay their ransom, as he believed that they were trying to swindle him. Eventually, the captain took the Landers onboard, and the brothers finally returned to England in 1831. Richard Lander was the first explorer to be honored with a medal by the Royal Geographical Society.

Europeans promptly attempted to use the Niger to build trade networks in the African interior. The British established a permanent trading outpost at Lokoja, where the Benue runs into the Niger, but it proved very difficult to keep the outpost staffed. As with Park's second expedition, many Europeans died of diseases such as malaria and dysentery in the so-called white man's grave. The death rate of Europeans in tropical Africa would significantly diminish only after the 1850s, when a medicine that combats malaria, called quinine, became more widely available. The discovery of quinine was essential to subsequent geographical discoveries.

A CITY OF GOLD TURNED TO MUD

If a European of the early 19th century could name one city in West Africa, that city would probably be Timbuktu. For most Europeans, and even for most expert geographers, Timbuktu represented the commercial prospects of the Niger. Although Europeans had reached Timbuktu in living memory, not one had survived to return home, due to the dangers of the Sahara Desert, disease, or the Tuaregs, Muslim marauders who patrolled the desert to prey upon caravans. After centuries of conflict between the Muslims of North Africa and the Christians of Europe, the Tuaregs showed no mercy to Christians who crossed their path. In 1826 a British army officer, Alexander Laing, had reached Timbuktu after nearly being killed by Tuaregs who had discovered that he was a Christian. He had been shot, his jaw had been broken, he had been slashed with knives, his right hand was nearly severed, and yet somehow he recovered in Timbuktu and managed to join a caravan traveling to Tripoli. Having come so far, Laing was then strangled to death under the orders of a Tuareg who captured him in the desert. His papers were promptly destroyed, and the news of his murder reached Tripoli months later.

The dangers of travel to Timbuktu made this destination irresistible to European geographers, businessmen, and explorers, who imagined that such dangers must have guarded a great prize. The Paris Geographical Society offered a reward of 10,000 francs to any European who could reach Timbuktu and return alive. This opportunity was quickly taken up by René Caillié, a young Frenchman who had been orphaned as a child and apprenticed to a shoemaker. Caillié had already given up the shoe business, having been inspired to travel by his reading of *Robinson Crusoe,* a novel by Daniel Defoe about the adventures of a seaman shipwrecked in the Pacific. He had gained experience in Africa by working as a servant to a French officer who was posted to Senegal, where the officer promptly died of fever. Not to be dissuaded, Caillié then joined three failed British expeditions up the Gambia River. He observed that these expeditions were regularly delayed by demands for gifts by local chiefs and that the many supplies that accompanied the expeditions attracted innumerable thieves. He therefore decided that he would be better off traveling alone than in a large caravan.

Caillié walked into the African interior in 1824 with a bundle of presents on his head. He proceeded up the Senegal River and then traveled overland until he encountered a Muslim people called the Brakna. He informed the chief that he had come to abandon his Christian faith and learn about Islam. Moreover, Caillié intended to learn how to live like an African and observe African customs in order to make his future travels possible. After living with the Brakna, he returned to the coast to gather more gifts, then set out again in 1827, this time bound for Timbuktu. He rejected the caravan route from Tripoli and instead began his approach to Timbuktu from present-day Guinea. He traveled alone, disguised as an Egyptian Arab. He explained that as a boy he had been enslaved by Europeans, who had recently released him on the West African coast to make his way home. On the strength of his knowledge of Islam, his familiarity with African customs, and his peculiar story, Caillié succeeded in joining a caravan headed north. He enjoyed good relations with both his caravan and the African peoples whom they met on the road. His only serious difficulty was a terrible case of fever that incapacitated him for the last

several months of 1827. Fortunately, an old woman in the town of Ségala agreed to care for him in his delirious state, and so he lay for months upon a mat on her floor. After recovering from his fever, he joined a slave caravan, which reached the Niger in April 1828. The caravan proceeded downstream for a couple of weeks, then left the river's fertile shores to enter a plain of white sand. About eight miles onward, they encountered Timbuktu. Caillié recounts in his travel memoir, *Travels through Central Africa to Timbuktoo:* "On entering this mysterious city, which is an object of curiosity and research to the civilized nations of Europe, I experienced an indescribable satisfaction. I was obliged, however, to restrain my feelings, and to God alone did I confide my joy." After passing through a state of euphoria, he next experienced keen disappointment.

> . . . I looked around and found that the sight before me did not answer my expectations. I had formed a totally different idea of the grandeur and wealth of Timbuktu. The city presented, at first view, nothing but a mass of ill-looking houses, built of earth. Nothing was to be seen in all directions but immense plains of quicksand of a yellowish white colour. The sky was a pale red as far as the horizon: all nature wore a dreary aspect, and the most profound silence prevailed; not even the warbling of a bird was to be heard. . . .

Caillié stayed with a wealthy merchant, Sidi-Abdallahi. The ruler and the majority of the population of Timbuktu were Africans of the Kissor people, but many Moroccans such as Sidi-Abdallah lived in the city as merchants. After a night's rest, Caillié walked around town and found little of the fabulous wealth that he had been led to expect. He saw camel caravans passing through the city and people asleep in the doorways of their homes. In the shops he saw a variety of European goods, including glassware and shotguns. Timbuktu was clearly a prosperous market, but it was not a city of gold. Caillié had an interview

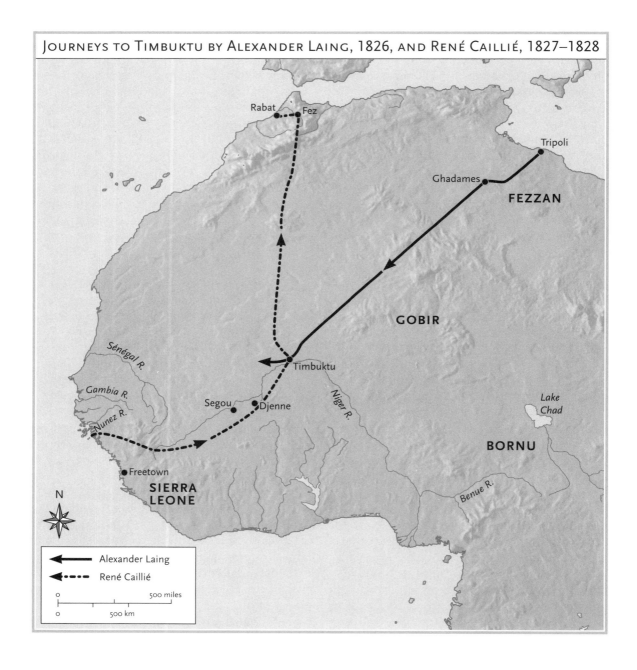

JOURNEYS TO TIMBUKTU BY ALEXANDER LAING, 1826, AND RENÉ CAILLIÉ, 1827–1828

The Geographical Societies

Today many nations, states, and even cities have their own geographical societies. The appearance and development of geographical societies took place in the 19th century. The first such organization, the Geographical Society of Paris, was founded in 1821. The Berlin Geographical Society was founded in 1828, and the precursor of the Royal Geographical Society was then founded in London in 1830. This was not just a European phenomenon. Geographical societies were established in Mexico (1833) and Brazil (1838) before the founding of the Imperial Russian Geographical Society in 1845. The founding of the American Geographical and Statistical Society in New York in 1851 was the first of many such societies in North America. Over the next few decades, societies would also be founded in Asia, such as the Tokyo Geographical Society in 1879. The primary objectives of the geographical societies were to distribute geographical knowledge, to support geographers and explorers in their work, and to honor their accomplishments.

These societies were not only produced by exploration and discovery, which had proceeded for ages beforehand. They were also the products of a combination of factors particular to exploration in the age of empire in the 19th century. They reflected the scientific priorities of modern exploration and the increasing identification of exploration as a national endeavor. The growing middle class, where national identity was strongest, filled the memberships in these societies in order to advance their interests in science, commerce, and humanitarianism—or simply to enhance their social status through identification with a noble cause. When explorers returned from major discoveries in the 19th century—in contrast to the 15th century—they would most often announce their findings to their nation's geographical society, and only later meet with their monarch.

with the king, who asked him about the Christians of Europe and the manner in which they had treated him. The king, like most others in the city, treated the Egyptian with kindness and generosity. "When I was at the mosque," Caillié recalls, "a middle-aged Moor stepped up to me gravely, and without saying a word slipped a handful of cowries into the pocket of my coussabe. He withdrew immediately, without affording me time to thank him. I was much surprised at this delicate way of giving alms."

Having gained a favorable impression of Timbuktu, Caillié departed northward across the Sahara with a caravan. The Sahara proved to be more dangerous than the jungles of West Africa, with its marauders, deadly sandstorms, and jackals lurking on the edge of the camp each night. After further trials and tribulations, he reached the French consulate at Tangier, from which he sailed home to France. He duly received the reward of 10,000 francs from the Paris Geographical Society and, in 1830, published his travel memoir. In the same year, France seized control of Algeria, making a decisive bid for imperial power in Africa. Henceforth, France would take a leading role in the exploration of the northeast regions of the continent.

Of the many Europeans who followed Caillié to Timbuktu, the most ambitious was Heinrich Barth, a German. Unlike Caillié, Barth took a remarkably long route to Timbuktu, covering approximately 10,000 miles. Barth was a geographer who spoke Arabic and was widely traveled in North Africa before his greatest exploratory journey. This journey began when he accompanied the British Central Africa Expedition in 1850, under the leadership of James Richardson. Although Richardson intended primarily to investigate the African slave trade, Barth and the other European member of the expedition, a German astronomer and geologist named Adolf Overweg, had scientific priorities. They departed from Tripoli and crossed the Sahara, after which they split up to pursue separate objectives. Richardson and Overweg soon died of disease, but Barth continued his explorations for another five years. He was the first European to visit the city of Agades in the southern Sahara, from which he proceeded in January 1851 to Tasawa. His wanderings then took him over vast stretches of terrain between Tripoli, Lake Chad, and Timbuktu. He was the first European to explore thoroughly Lake Chad and the upper reaches of the Benue River, which the Landers had seen flow into the Niger.

Barth was able to travel widely because he succeeded in keeping dangerous company. At various points he traveled with Arab marauders, and once he accompanied a military expedition by the ruler of Kukawa against his subjects in the kingdom of Mandara. This was a ferocious expedition, during which Barth witnessed thousands of Africans taken into slavery and hundreds more slaughtered or mutilated. He finally reached Timbuktu in 1853, then returned to Britain to publish *Travels and Discoveries in North and Central Africa, 1849–55*. In addition to making many other novel observations, Barth explained that Caillié had underestimated the wealth of Timbuktu because he had not been aware that the city had been attacked by a hostile tribe in the year before his visit.

THE SOURCE OF THE NILE

The Nile River flows more than 4,000 miles northward from central Africa to the Mediterranean Sea. Europeans had been aware of the river for thousands of years, because of its position near important trade routes and the great empires of ancient Egypt that grew up along its banks. Europeans did not know where the river originated, though historians, including Herodotus, and geographers had long speculated that it must flow from a massive, inland lake. In the 1770s a Scot named James Bruce traveled to Abyssinia in northeast Africa in order to locate the source of the Nile. Instead, he spent three eventful years in the court of Tekle Haimanot II, the emperor of Abyssinia, and found the source of the so-called Blue Nile, a major tributary of the larger river, known as the White Nile. Although Bruce's explorations were regarded as worthwhile scientific inquiries, Europeans suddenly found tremendous strategic importance in the Nile when the French armies of Napoleon Bonaparte invaded Egypt in 1798. Although Bonaparte's invasion stalled before it could extend beyond Egypt's borders, he made clear his desire to proceed eastward to conquer the Asian empires of Russia and Great Britain. Napoleon's arrival in Egypt conveyed to both the British and Russian Empires that Egypt was a key to the security of their Asian possessions, and they further understood that the Nile was the key to the livelihood and security of Egypt. By the middle of the 19th century, the security of Egypt became all the more important when the European powers commenced planning and building the Suez Canal, which would cut through Egypt to connect the Mediterranean and the Red Seas in 1869.

Missionaries in East Africa reported after the 1840s that they had heard from Africans about a great inland body of water and snow-capped mountains along the equator. If this lake and these mountains existed, thought European geographers, they would provide a likely source for the Nile River. Consequently, in 1856, the Royal Geographical Society sponsored an expedition to find the inland lake and mountains, and hopefully the source of the Nile, from the East African coast. This expedition was to be led by Richard Burton and accompanied by John Hanning Speke, men with a record of disastrous explorations behind them.

Both Burton and Speke had served as officers in the Army of India. Speke had joined the Indian army in 1844 and seen combat in the Punjab in the north of the country. It must be

The Nile River flows northward from the place in the Sudan where two rivers—the Blue and White Niles—meet. This early-20th-century photograph captures a few people and a camel along the banks of the Nile River, with the Egyptian pyramids in the distance. *(Library of Congress, Prints and Photographs Division [LC-USZ62-118798])*

said that Speke's primary interest in exploration was big-game hunting, in contrast to Burton, who was an accomplished geographer and linguist. Burton and Speke undertook their first exploratory journey together in Somalia in 1854, where they were ambushed one night in their tents at Berbera by the Habr Owel tribe. Burton had a spear thrown through his cheeks, taking with it four of his teeth. Speke was captured and eventually escaped, having been wounded 11 times. With their supplies stolen or destroyed, and many

Richard Burton, shown in this late-19th-century engraving, and John Hanning Speke led an expedition sponsored by the Royal Geographical Society to locate the Nile River's source. Speke found and named Lake Victoria, but he and Burton disagreed about its connection to the Nile. *(Library of Congress, Prints and Photographs Division [LC-USZ61-236])*

of their servants in flight, Burton and Speke abandoned their expedition and returned to England. But in 1857 they were off again to East Africa, now under the auspices of the Royal Geographical Society, to find the source of the Nile.

In June the two men and a column of over a hundred porters set off from the coastal town of Bagamoyo, one of the most common departure points for European expeditions into central Africa. They immediately encountered difficulties, the most dangerous of which was disease. After a couple of months, Speke was almost blind, and his efforts to kill a beetle that had crawled into his ear while he slept had left him deaf in one ear. Burton had also lost much of his sight, and he could no longer walk due to the paralysis of his legs. The two men nonetheless became the first Europeans to encounter Lake Tanganyika. Unfortunately, they could barely see it, and they were unable to explore its shores. The local African tribes told them that the lake had an outlet to the north, but Burton and Speke could not discern whether this outlet flowed out or in. In fact, this issue would not be settled until Henry Morton Stanley and David Livingstone circumnavigated the lake in 1872.

Burton and Speke decided to return to the coast in order to recover their health. On the way eastward, Speke regained his strength and much of his sight, though Burton remained incapacitated. They heard reports of a great lake to the north, a lake so large that no one knew its length or breadth. Both Africans and Muslim traders simply referred to this body of water as the N'yanza, "the lake," with no further need to distinguish it from the many other bodies of water in the region. Speke received Burton's permission to undertake a short investigation of this lake on his own. According to Speke's account, *What*

Led to the Discovery of the Source of the Nile, he saw the southern tip of the lake from a distance on July 30, 1858, and he then gained his first full view of the lake on August 3. Speke recalled that he reached the summit of a hill, "when the vast expanse of the pale-blue waters of the N'yanza burst suddenly upon my gaze." It appeared to him an inland sea, and he was unable to determined the distances of the shores.

> This view was one which, even in a well-known and explored country, would have arrested the traveler by its peaceful beauty. The islands, each swelling in a gentle slope to a rounded summit, clothed in wood between the rugged angular closely-cropping rocks of granite, seemed mirrored in the calm surface of the lake; on which I here and there detected a small black speck, the tiny canoe of some Muanza fisherman. . . . The pleasure of the mere view vanished in the presence of those more intense and exciting emotions which are called up by the consideration of the commercial and geographical importance of the prospect before me.

Speke immediately concluded, with no specific evidence, that this lake must be the legendary source of the Nile. He stated, "I no longer felt any doubt that the lake at my feet gave birth to that interesting river, the source of which has been the subject of so much speculation, and the object of so many explorers." To commemorate this discovery, Speke decided to name the lake Victoria, after the British queen, and he then hurried back to convey this exciting news to Burton, who had no hesitation in rejecting Speke's claim. Burton refused to believe that the Nile flowed from a lake that he had never seen, and he would continue to dispute this issue with

Speke for several years. Burton asserted that the Nile probably originated from Lake Tanganyika, a lake that, by no coincidence, he had taken a hand in discovering.

In an effort to settle the matter, the Royal Geographical Society sent Speke back to Lake Victoria in 1860, accompanied this time by James Augustus Grant. They proceeded north along the lake and became the first Europeans to enter the African kingdom of Buganda, ruled by Kabaka Mtesa, in 1862. Once more traveling alone, Speke proceeded to the northern end of the lake and was told by the Waganda people that he would indeed find a river leaving the lake at what they called "the stones." These stones turned out to be a waterfall. In his *Journal of the Discovery of the Source of the Nile,* Speke described the falls as about 12 feet high and 400 to 500 feet across, broken by rocks.

> It was a sight that attracted one to it for hours—the roar of the waters, the thousands of passenger fish, leaping at the falls with all their might; the Wasoga and Waganda fishermen coming out in boats and taking posts on all the rocks with rod and hook, hippopotami and crocodiles lying sleepily on the water, the ferry at work above the falls, and cattle driven down to drink on the margin of the lake—made, in all, with the pretty nature of the country—small hills, grassy topped, with trees in the folds, and gardens on the lower slopes—as interesting a picture as one could wish to see.

Speke renamed "the stones" the Ripon Falls, after the man who had presided over the Royal Geographical Society when his expedition was first organized. "The expedition had now performed its functions," Speke concluded. "I saw that old father Nile without any doubt rises in the Victoria N'yanza, and, as I had foretold, that lake is the great source of the holy river which cradled the first expounder of our religious belief."

Speke returned to meet Grant and informed him of his discovery at the northern end of the lake. Unfortunately, the men recognized that they no longer had the supplies necessary to follow the river downstream. Moreover, they were unable to investigate reports of another outlet in the northeast corner of the lake leading to another lake beyond. Having to content themselves with finding the

Porters and Captains

European explorers were dependent upon African porters to conduct large expeditions. In the era before the construction of railways in Africa, one could only move large quantities of goods on the backs of pack animals or people. In West Africa Europeans quickly discovered that diseases and the climate weakened them and their animals to such an extent that neither could survive bearing heavy loads over long distances. In East Africa, the tsetse fly was a deadly threat to livestock, making human porters the only reliable mode of transportation.

As many expeditions into central Africa departed from the east, a ready workforce of porters developed on the island of Zanzibar, the major port in the region, and at the coastal town of Bagamoyo, from which expeditions followed ancient caravan routes into the interior. The most common porters in the last half of the 19th century were the Wangwana of Zanzibar and the Wanyamwezi of the region around Lake Victoria. Henry Stanley observes in *Through the Dark Continent:* "It is to the Wangwana that Livingstone, Burton, Speke and Grant owe, in great part, the accomplishment of their objects, and while in the employ of these explorers, this race rendered great services to geography." He then notes that the Wanyamwezi are superior as porters, though not as advanced in other respects. "Their greater freedom from diseases, their great strength and endurance, the pride they take in their profession as porters, prove them born travelers of incalculable use and benefit in Africa."

Porters were paid in accordance with their experience and skill. It was customary to provide porters with an advance of three or four months on their wages, which the porters could then pass on to their families before their departure. The work of the common porter was straightforward. He was to carry a load, which might consist of gifts for local rulers, cloth, metalwork, and other articles for trade, or ammunition. Desertions from the column were a common occurrence, as were deaths along the trail due to disease, injury, or an attack by a hostile people or robbers. In 1862 Speke left for Lake Victoria with 176 men, but arrived in Egypt with only 18. This rate of attrition was by no means unusual.

The success of an expedition depended largely upon the Africans chosen to "captain" the porters. A good captain served not only as a manager but also as

Ripon Falls, Speke and Grant traveled overland to reconnect with the Nile farther north and then catch a boat to the town of Khartoum. Imagine their surprise when they returned to the Nile at Gondokoro and met Speke's old friend, Samuel Baker, accompanied by a young European woman named Florenz or Florence von Sass.

The two were as unlikely a couple as one might hope to meet in central Africa. Baker was a gentleman of independent wealth who enjoyed traveling and hunting. He had been

a negotiator with local chiefs, as a translator, and as a guide. One of the most famous of the African captains was Bombay, a freed slave who was serving in the army of Said Burgash, the sultan of Zanzibar when he met Speke. Speke recruited Bombay to join him and Burton in their expedition to discover the source of the Nile, and Speke then hired him again to return with him and Grant to Lake Victoria. Like other successful captains, Bombay's services were sought by subsequent explorers. Stanley hired Bombay to captain his search for Livingstone in 1871, and Cameron hired Bombay to captain his transcontinental journey in 1874. In 1876 the Royal Geographical Society awarded Bombay a pension that he enjoyed until his death in 1884.

Explorers of Africa such as Richard Burton, John Hanning Speke, and David Livingstone depended on porters to carry supplies, gifts, ammunition, and anything else they needed. *(Library of Congress, Prints and Photographs Division [LC-USZ62-108546])*

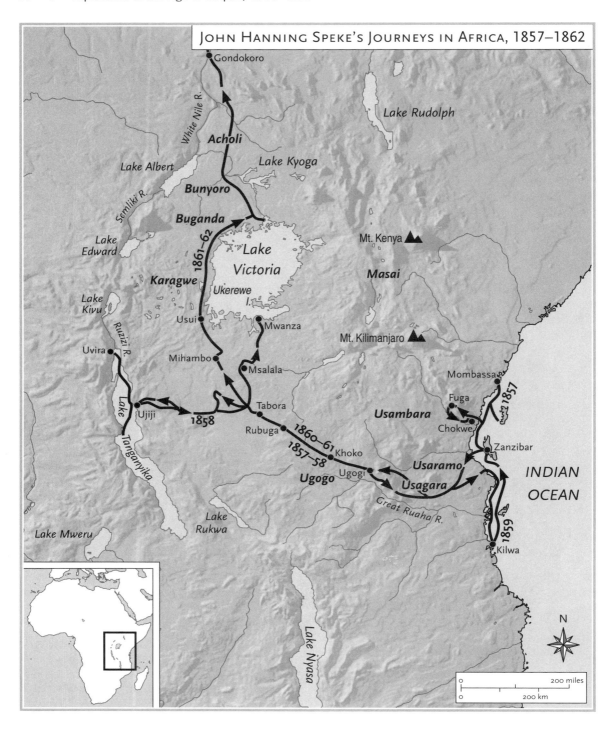

JOHN HANNING SPEKE'S JOURNEYS IN AFRICA, 1857–1862

married, but his wife had died, leaving him in his mid-30s with four children. He had placed these children in the care of his wife's sister, then set out from Britain to hunt wild boar and other game in eastern Europe and Asia. During these journeys, he had found himself at Widdin, a fortress of the Ottoman Empire in present-day Bulgaria, where he saw a group of Hungarians up for sale at a slave auction. Among this group was a 15-year-old, blonde-haired woman who caught Baker's attention, probably because of her youthful beauty. Baker purchased the woman, and they subsequently fell in love. Given the peculiar origin of their relationship, Baker did not mention Florence to his family in Britain, and he delayed his return home year after year. In the course of these delays, he became intrigued by the idea of finding the source of the Nile, and so he organized an expedition to this end.

Samuel and Florence set off up the Nile from Cairo in 1861. They left their boat at Korosko and then rode camels across the Nubian Desert. They explored the rivers leading into the Blue Nile, then proceeded to Khartoum in order to travel up the White Nile. They reached Gondokoro, which Samuel Baker described as "a perfect hell," filled with cutthroats who made their living selling slaves, guns, and liquor. Under the influence of the locals, the men in the Bakers' expedition became unruly. At one point, Samuel Baker confronted the ringleader of the expedition's malcontents on the dock beside their boat, resulting in an open brawl and the possibility of a general mutiny. While Samuel fought to restore order, Florence emerged from the boat and pushed her way through the fight, yelling at the men to stand back. Florence's courage was greeted with stunned silence by the men, and she then negotiated a tactful settlement that enabled both Samuel and his adversaries to save face. Florence would continue to intervene on Samuel's behalf throughout the expedition, displaying a greater gift for diplomacy than the short-tempered Samuel.

As Samuel and Florence prepared to depart upriver, they heard guns firing in the distance. Samuel Baker recalls the scene in his journal, published subsequently in his travel memoir, *Albert N'Yanza:*

> Guns firing in the distance; Debono's ivory porters arriving, for whom I have waited. My men rushed madly to my boat, with a report that two white men were with them who had come from the sea! Could they be Speke and Grant? Off I ran, and soon met them in reality; hurrah for old England!! They had come from the Victorian Nyanza, from which the Nile springs . . . The mystery of ages solved.

Baker was naturally disappointed that his own objective had already been achieved, but Speke and Grant then told him about the lake to the west of Victoria. Grant even provided Samuel and Florence with a map, which proved generally accurate. Samuel Baker stated, "Speke expressed his conviction that the Luta N'zige must be a second source of the Nile, and that geographers would be dissatisfied that he had not explored it. To me this was most gratifying." Samuel and Florence accordingly organized their large expedition, which carried nearly three tons of supplies and gifts toward the rumored lake. They joined a merchant caravan and, despite serious problems with the discipline of their porters, traveled 180 miles overland. In the midst of the journey, when the caravan was crossing a river, Samuel looked back to see Florence drop into the reeds, as if shot dead. She had suddenly contracted a fever, which left her unconscious and then delirious for several days. The caravan could not stop due to lack of food, so Florence was carried forward on a litter. Samuel sat up each night to watch her for any sign of recovery, but her condition appeared hopeless. It was only after the African porters had begun to assemble tools to dig her grave that Florence regained consciousness and, slowly, her strength. The caravan pressed on, and with the assistance of

a chief named Kamrasi, Samuel and Florence finally reached the lake in March 1864.

They emerged from the forest about 1,500 feet above the lake, then descended on a zigzag path for about two hours. Although weakened by fever, Florence insisted on walking this final stretch to the lake with Samuel, clinging to his arm for balance. "A walk of about a mile through flat sandy meadows of

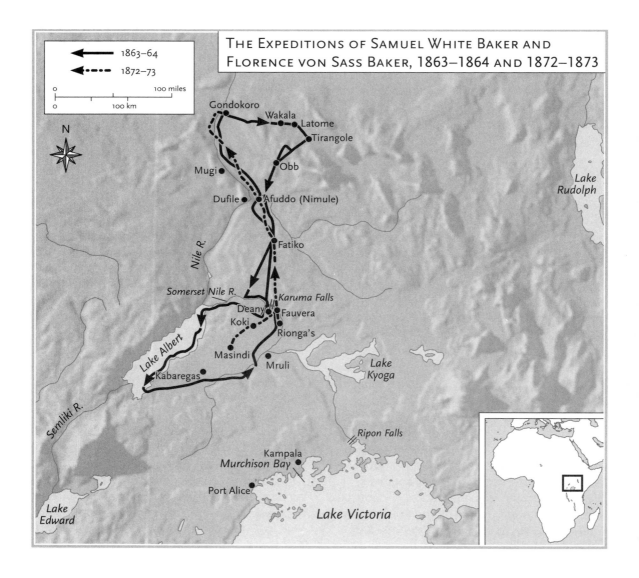

THE EXPEDITIONS OF SAMUEL WHITE BAKER AND FLORENCE VON SASS BAKER, 1863–1864 AND 1872–1873

fine turf interspersed with trees and bush, brought us to the water's edge," Samuel Baker recalled. "The waves were rolling upon a white pebbly beach: I rushed into the lake, and thirsty with heat and fatigue, with a heart full of gratitude, I drank deeply from the Sources of the Nile."

> No European foot had ever trod upon its sand, nor had the eyes of a white man ever scanned its vast expanse of water. We were the first; and this was the key to the great secret that even Julius Caesar yearned to unravel, but in vain. Here was the great basin of the Nile that received *every drop of water,* even from the passing shower to the roaring mountain torrent that drained from Central Africa towards the north. This was the great reservoir of the Nile!

Samuel Baker named it Lake Albert, in honor of the husband of Queen Victoria.

Samuel and Florence were both struck down by fever at Lake Albert. In view of their dwindling supplies and in order to save their lives, they departed for home, leaving one geographical question unanswered. It appeared that a river flowing into Lake Albert from the northeast was the Nile, but they were not certain, and there was another river leaving the lake from the west. This matter would be later settled by an American, Charles Chaillé-Long. In the service of the Egyptian army in the 1870s, he was sent on a mission to Buganda. He then returned via the Ripon Falls, tracking 100 miles of the uncharted Nile, proving that the Nile entered and left Lake Albert.

In the meantime, Samuel and Florence returned to Cairo, where Samuel found correspondence awaiting him at the British consulate. Among the various letters was one from the Royal Geographical Society, inform-

ing him that he has been awarded the Victoria Gold Medal. The couple was married in London in November 1865, and Samuel was knighted in 1866. Given the unseemly background of Baker's wife, Queen Victoria would not permit him to bring her to the ceremony. Florence nevertheless became Lady Baker, and she returned with Samuel to Africa between 1869 and 1873 to abolish the slave trade. The ruler of Egypt appointed Baker the governor-general of the Equatorial Nile Basin and financed his four-year expedition against slavery. As Baker declares in *Albert N'Yanza:*

> Slavery murders the sacred feeling of love, that blessing that cheers the lot of the poorest man, that spell that binds him to his wife, and child, and home. . . . Thus is Africa accursed: nor can she be raised to any scale approaching to civilization until the slave-trade shall be totally suppressed. The first step necessary to the improvement of the savage tribes of the White Nile is the annihilation of the slave-trade. Until this be effected, no legitimate commerce can be established; neither is there an opening for missionary enterprise;—the country is sealed and closed against all improvement.

SEEKING REDEMPTION ON THE NILE

Dr. David Livingstone had been made famous by his travels across Africa, but in 1864 he returned to Britain with his reputation tarnished. For several years he had led an expedition up the Zambezi River that was, by all accounts, a complete failure. Now he was looking for a new destination. He found it at Bath, a British resort town where, in September 1864, he was to give a lecture and attend a much-publicized debate over the source of the Nile by two of the other prominent explorers of the mid-19th century, Burton and Speke. Unfortunately, the debate never took place, because Speke was shot dead just beforehand in what appeared to be a hunting accident. With the debate unresolved, Livingstone recognized that the source of the Nile remained the most important geographical question of his time, and therefore a question worthy of his attention. Perhaps Livingstone also thought that by discovering the source of the Nile he might redeem his reputation following the debacle on the Zambezi. Setting aside the theories of Burton and Speke, Livingstone speculated that the source of the Nile must be farther south, in the Lualaba River. With financial support from the British government and James Young, the inventor of paraffin, Livingstone set out from Britain on his last expedition in 1865. He departed from the east coast of Africa into the interior in the following year, never to find the source of the Nile and never to return.

Livingstone was soon followed by Verney Lovett Cameron, who explored Lake Tanganyika and found that its outlet flowed into the Lukaga River, rather than the Nile. He then arrived at the Lualaba in August 1874 and proceeded downstream to Nyangwe, the same place where Livingstone had turned back from his quest for the source of the Nile in 1870. Again, the local merchants refused to provide a European explorer with canoes. As Cameron continued to negotiate at Nyangwe, he also took measurements of the river's altitude that enabled him to prove that the Lualaba could not be the source of the Nile. It was simple: The elevation of the Lualaba in the area of Nyangwe was lower than the lowest point of the Nile, and one could not reasonably argue that the Lualaba flowed uphill. Having refuted Livingstone's theory, Cameron concluded that the Lualaba was probably the source of the Congo River to the west. Henry

Stanley would subsequently confirm Cameron's finding that the Tanganyika could not be the source of the Nile and show that the Lualaba River flowed not into the Nile, but the Congo, when he reached the mouth of the Congo River in 1877.

The European explorations of the Niger and Nile Rivers had important consequences for the peoples of Africa in both the near and the long term. In the near term, European travel to and along these rivers confirmed the ongoing brutalities of the slave trade and provoked European governments to take further action to stop it. Also, the large expeditions of Burton, Speke, Grant, and Stanley helped to create a new and profitable form of work for Africans. An increasing number of Africans would become porters and captains, expanding the interaction between African peoples and drawing Africans to the caravan routes and their major stations, such as Bagamoyo on the east coast. In the long term, the explorations of the Niger and the Nile opened paths for Europeans into the African interior, where Europeans built their trade and established missionary stations to spread the Christian faith. Greater access to the African interior produced greater competition and aggression between Europeans and indigenous rulers, and between Europeans themselves. In 1882, for example, the British used their naval power to establish their control over Egypt, which the Suez Canal had transformed into the primary sea route to Asia. At the end of the century, in 1898, Britain and France almost went to war for control of the upper Nile, upon which the welfare of the lower Nile depended.

Europe's expansion down the Niger and up the Nile was not merely a process of economic exploitation, religious conversion, and conquest. Additionally, as European imperialists stabilized their authority in these regions, they were followed by professional and ama-

Portions of the Nile River, especially the area of the Nile River valley, have steep banks of granite. *(Library of Congress, Prints and Photographs Division [LC-USZ62-127967])*

teur scientists, and particularly, in Egypt, by archaeologists. These researchers located, unearthed, and documented the tombs, temples, and cities of the ancient Egyptian kings and queens, laying the foundations for the field of Egyptology. Unfortunately, these scientists found themselves competing against grave robbers and others who would turn a profit by plundering and selling ancient artifacts to private collectors in Europe. One of the most successful champions of ancient Egypt's legacy proved to be a British woman, Amelia Edwards, who was a writer of short stories and novels before her first and only trip to Egypt in 1873–74. Edwards was inspired and awed by the Egyptian monuments that she saw and alarmed by the evidence of their destruction. Consequently, upon her return, she published a well-received travel memoir, *A Thousand Miles up the Nile*, and pushed, prodded, and organized an influential group of scientists and museum curators to found the Egypt Exploration Society, which is still at work today funding scientific excavations and the preservation of the monuments of ancient Egypt. Indeed, the society reveals the simultaneously destructive and constructive influences of empire in exploration. The society was, after all, founded in 1882, the same year in which Britain began its conquest of Egypt with a naval bombardment of the ancient port city of Alexandria.

5

TAMING THE
HEART OF DARKNESS

 Joseph Conrad's novella *Heart of Darkness,* published in 1899, opens on the river Thames in England, where several men wait aboard a boat for the tide to carry them out to sea. As the dusk falls, one of the men, Charlie Marlow, begins to tell a tale about his earlier travels in central Africa. He recalls that as a boy he looked at maps of the world and dreamed of traveling to the blank spaces. Africa had been the biggest of those blank spaces during his childhood, but that had changed by the end of the century. "It had filled since my boyhood with rivers and lakes and names," Marlow observes. "It had ceased to be a blank space of delightful mystery—a white patch for a boy to dream gloriously over. It had become a place of darkness."

In the 19th century every schoolchild had heard of the forbidden place known then to many as the "Dark Continent." Most people identified Africa not with the Muslim lands north of the Sahara Desert or with the arid regions of the south, but with its heart: a vast region of great lakes, rivers, and dense jungle.

Central Africa was a place of myth and mystery in the minds of Europeans, who imagined a place overrun by wild beasts, cannibals, and slave traders. To them it represented all that was uncivilized, all that was savage. And it also represented hope, or at least hopeful, tantalizing prospects for future profits, conversions to the Christian faith, and adventure. Children dreamt of Africa, and some grew up to become explorers who cut through Africa's jungles and rode down its rivers in canoes. These explorers commonly spoke of carrying commerce and Christianity in a benevolent "civilizing mission" to Africans. As they advanced, however, their optimism and their confidence were hard to sustain as myths gave way to realities. Europeans took far more from central Africa than they gave in return, exploiting resources and labor in exchange, too often, for only liquor and guns, or for relief from conquest. By the end of the century, central Africa had, indeed, become a place of darkness, but a darkness of the European's making.

CROSSING AFRICA

Commerce and Christianity were, from the outset, the driving forces behind European exploration in central Africa. In the 1840s, Dr. David Livingstone, a member of the London Missionary Society in South Africa, decided that he must try to find a natural highway from the coastline into the interior, a highway on which missionary stations, trading factories, and perhaps, someday, colonial settlements might prosper. This highway would bring benefits both to Europeans and to Africans, for it would lead to the end of the slave trade. In Livingstone's travel memoir, *Missionary Travels and Researches in South Africa,* he explains: "If the slave market were supplied with articles of European manufacture by legitimate commerce, the trade in slaves would become impossible. . . . This could only be effected by establishing a highway from the coast into the centre of the country." In order to mark this highway, Livingstone intended, first and foremost, to establish a missionary outpost deep in the interior. In order to establish such a mission station, he had to find an area in central Africa that was free of malaria, the tsetse fly, and the slave trade. In the middle of the 19th century, Europeans had not yet found such a place, and they had no reason to believe that it existed.

Livingstone set out northward from Kolobeng, South Africa, in April 1850, accompanied in ox-drawn wagons by his wife and three children; his fellow missionary, William Oswell; and a local chief, Sechele. Wagon-traveling, according to Livingstone, "is a prolonged system of picnicking, excellent for the health, and agreeable to those who are not over-fastidious about trifles, and who delight in being in the open air." They proceeded into the land of the Makololo, where they established excellent relations with the chief, Sebituane, who welcomed their proposal to establish a mission station in his kingdom. The chief died before he could assist Livingstone, but he was succeeded by his daughter, Mamochisane, who intended to honor her father's wishes. With this new chief's blessing, Livingstone's small expedition proceeded into central Africa, arriving at Sesheke in June 1851. There they came upon a surprising sight: the Zambezi River, one of the great rivers of Africa. "This was an important point," Livingstone observes, "for that river was not previously known to exist there at all." It was the dry season, but the width of river was 300 to 600 yards of deep water. The region around Sesheke was marshy and fever-ridden, but the local people lived there because the inhospitable land provided protection from slave traders. Livingstone suspected that farther upriver he might find a more suitable area for his missionary station, which would also serve as a way station on the commercial highway that the Zambezi offered into the interior. Livingstone recalls, "I at once resolved to save my family from exposure to this unhealthy region by sending them to England, and to return alone, with a view to exploring the country in search of a healthy district that might prove a centre of civilization, and open up the interior by a path to either the east or west coast."

Livingstone returned to Cape Town and sent his family home. He wasted no time in setting off northward from the Cape in June 1852, accompanied by a small number of African servants in ox wagons. He returned to the land of the Makololo, where he again enjoyed a generous reception, this time from both Mamochisane and a new chief, an 18-year-old man named Sekelutu. With Sekelutu's support, Livingstone returned to Sesheke and embarked up the Zambezi with 33 canoes. He proceeded easily through

Makololo territory, enjoying the patronage of a series of chiefs, including another female chief named Manenko. His good fortune continued until early in 1854, when he left the upper reaches of the Zambezi and crossed the watershed between the Zambezi and the Congo Rivers.

He had not yet found an area suitable for a mission station, but he was still hopeful that he might find one if he proceeded west. He encountered two black Portuguese slave traders, Silva Porto and Caetano Ferra, who told him about a route followed by slave caravans to Luanda, Angola, in West Africa. Livingstone followed this route, but he soon suffered from the fear and hostility that slave traders had created along the way. As he and his expedition followed the slave route through both jungle and desolate terrain, he had to buy all of his food from local chiefs, who became increasingly demanding and belligerent as he traveled west. Livingstone had particular problems in the country of the Chiboque, a people who had the disconcerting custom of filing their teeth to sharp points, which Livingstone regarded as evidence of their cannibalism. The expedition finally made it to Cassange, a Portuguese outpost, where the officers fed and clothed Livingstone and his men and provided them with a guide to the coast. The final march was arduous, and Livingstone was nearly killed by hunger and fever as he staggered to the coast. He probably would have died had it not been for a ship's surgeon who cared for him and put him back on this feet after several weeks. The Europeans at Luanda and along the West African coast hailed Livingstone's heroism, and the news of his expedition made headlines in British newspapers. Nevertheless, Livingstone perceived that his work was not finished. He had not yet succeeded in finding an area suitable for a mission station, and he had not found a

safe route into the African interior. To the amazement of his European hosts at Luanda, he resupplied his expedition and returned east.

Livingstone reached the upper Zambezi in 1855 and once more benefited from the hospitality of the Makololo. His expedition traveled down the Zambezi in canoes, until they heard about nearby lands which were reputed to be rich in vegetation and wildlife, and free from malaria, the tsetse fly, and even the slave trade. These lands were occupied by the Batoka, who were the subjects of a Makololo chief. Livingstone promptly left the river to investigate, guided by a few Batoka men. The Batoka led Livingstone to a plateau about 1,000 miles from the coast, where Livingstone was elated to discover excellent prospects for a mission station. The Batoka informed him, "No one ever dies of hunger here." Livingstone saw abundant game that had not yet learned to fear people, given that the Batoka did not possess firearms. Livingstone recalls his view from a hilltop:

> The plain below us . . . had more large game on it than any where else I had seen in Africa. Hundreds of buffaloes and zebras grazed on the open spaces, and there stood lordly elephants feeding majestically. . . . I wished that I had been able to take a photograph of a scene so seldom beheld, and which is destined, as guns increase, to pass away from the earth.

Livingstone also saw rich vegetation and soil that he regarded as suitable for grazing livestock or for farmlands. He regarded the Batoka people less favorably, for they were more savage, in Livingstone's opinion, than the Makololo. Livingstone was not impressed when Batoka leaders greeted him by rolling themselves naked in the dirt, and he was repulsed by the Batoka's custom of knocking out the front teeth of boys and girls at puberty, giving all of the people the appearance of old men. Despite his aversion to the Batoka's customs, Livingstone was certain that they, like all Africans, could be uplifted by the influences of commerce and Christianity.

Unfortunately, in his haste to carry news of the Batoka Plateau to the coast, Livingstone returned to the Zambezi at a point far to the east of where he had set off on foot for the plateau. He erroneously assumed that the river was navigable between these points, but, in fact, it was rendered impassable by a series of rapids that Livingstone had overlooked. He might easily have taken measurements of altitude on the river and determined that there was a drop that would certainly indicate either rapids or waterfalls. It appears that, after all his hardships, Livingstone was distracted for at least one fateful moment from the careful calculations that are essential to exploration. Contemplating his wishful vision of a mission station on the Batoka Plateau, he arrived at the mouth of the Zambezi in May 1856, having covered 5,000 miles and completed the first crossing of sub-Saharan Africa by a European. Silva Porto, one of the black Portuguese slave traders who had provided Livingstone's route to Luanda, had tried and failed to take the same route to the east coast in 1853. Two of Porto's African servants had succeeded, however, in beating Livingstone by three years.

FROM FAME IN BRITAIN TO FAILURE ON THE ZAMBEZI

Livingstone returned to Britain in late 1856 and received numerous honors and awards, including a gold medal from the Royal Geographical Society. His recent expedition was described as one of the greatest achievements in exploration in the modern era, as it certainly was. His findings were of interest to merchants and industrialists, who listened intently to his descriptions of the natural resources of Africa. Missionary societies would hereafter dream of building a chain of missions across central Africa. Among many other lectures, Livingstone gave a stirring talk at the Senate House at Cambridge University in 1857. He concluded this talk by declaring: "I go back to Africa to try to make an open path for commerce and Christianity; do you carry out the work which I have begun. I leave it to you!" Livingstone's rallying cry at Cambridge inspired the creation of the Universities' Mission to Central Africa. Many of the founding brethren of this mission would, indeed, not only follow Livingstone to Africa in the years ahead but also die for his misjudgment on the Zambezi.

Livingstone regarded exploration as essential to missionary expansion, but he found that the settled nature of the London Missionary Society was not suited to this form of evangelical work. Consequently, Livingstone left the mission in order to become a British consular official in 1858. The British government had an interest in Livingstone's exploration of the Zambezi, as this river was in the proximity of the British colony at Natal, on the east coast of South Africa, and was believed to offer access to the potential riches of central Africa. The government therefore agreed to finance Livingstone's return to the Zambezi River. Livingstone observes in his *Narrative of an Expedition to the Zambezi and Its Tributaries:*

> The main object of the Zambezi Expedition . . . was to extend the knowledge already attained of the geography and mineral and agricultural resources of Eastern

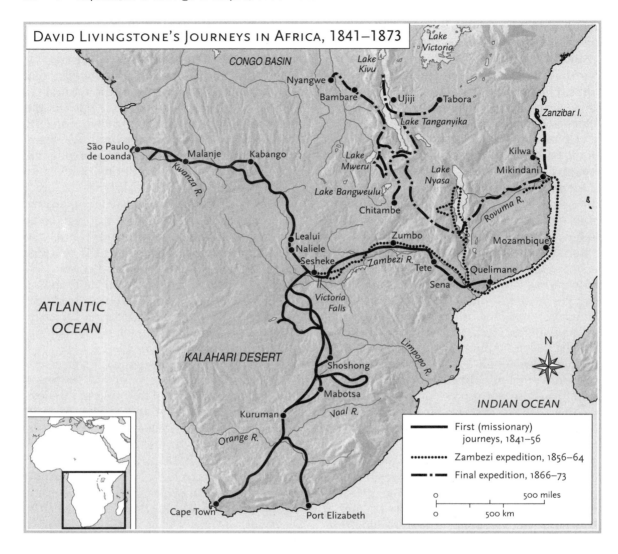

DAVID LIVINGSTONE'S JOURNEYS IN AFRICA, 1841–1873

CONGO BASIN

Lake Victoria

Lake Kivu

Nyangwe

Bambare

Ujiji

Tabora

Zanzibar I.

Lake Tanganyika

São Paulo de Loanda

Malanje

Kabango

Kwanza R.

Lake Mweru

Lake Nyasa

Kilwa

Mikindani

Lake Bangweulu

Chitambe

Rovuma R.

Lealui

Naliele

Sesheke

Zumbo

Mozambique

Zambezi R.

Tete

Quelimane

ATLANTIC OCEAN

Victoria Falls

Sena

KALAHARI DESERT

Limpopo R.

Shoshong

Mabotsa

N

Kuruman

Vaal R.

INDIAN OCEAN

Orange R.

First (missionary) journeys, 1841–56

Zambezi expedition, 1856–64

Final expedition, 1866–73

0   500 miles

0   500 km

Cape Town

Port Elizabeth

and Central Africa—to improve our acquaintance with the inhabitants, and to endeavor to engage them to apply themselves to industrial pursuits and to the cultivation of their lands with a view to the production of raw material to be exported to England in return for British manufacturers; and it was hoped that, by encouraging the natives to occupy themselves in the development of the resources of the country, a considerable advance might be made toward the extinction of the slave-trade, as they would not be long in discovering that the former would eventually be a more certain source of profit than the latter.

Although the official objectives of the expedition did not include the establishment of a mission station on the Batoka Plateau, this remained Livingstone's primary, personal motivation.

The expedition set off in 1858, accompanied by artists, scientists, and Livingstone's wife. It also included two photographers, Charles Livingstone—the explorer's brother—and John Kirk. The expedition proceeded up the Zambezi toward the Batoka Plateau, but it was stopped by the rapids that Livingstone had overlooked two years earlier. The expedition then experienced a series of calamities that were only made worse by Livingstone's refusal to quit. Livingstone's wife died of fever, and diseases overtook other members of the party. Given that the Zambezi was clearly not a highway into central Africa, and given that boats could not reach the vicinity of the Batoka Plateau, Livingstone began looking for another location for European settlement. He believed that he found such a place on the Shire River, which fed into the lower Zambezi, on elevated terrain that came to be called the Shire Highlands. Livingstone proposed that the British government establish a colony in the Highlands, but the government flatly refused, as it was not prepared to make the financial investment. Ignoring the interests of his government, Livingstone then invited the Universities Mission to establish a station in the Highlands. The mission sent its brethren, many of whom quickly died of disease. In 1863, Livingstone was still attempting to establish a settlement in the region of the Zambezi, but the government had finally lost all confidence in his judgment and cut off his funds. In January an editorial in *The Times* criticized Livingstone's Zambezi expedition as a failure and a waste of money: "We were promised cotton, sugar and indigo, and of course we got none. We were promised converts and not one has been made. In a word, the thousands subscribed have been productive only of the most fatal results."

A lesser explorer would have been ruined by this experience. Livingstone, however, was able to return to Britain and gather support for another expedition, this time in search of the source of the Nile River. He arrived in Africa in 1865 and died there in 1873. Despite Livingstone's long absence from Britain, he died at the height of his fame, which was

Adventure and exploration lured many men and women. David Livingstone's wife accompanied him on his 1858 expedition along the Zambezi River but died of fever early in the trip. Ida Pfeiffer, an Austrian woman, also felt the lure of adventure, and some of her journeys resulted in her 1854 book, *A Women's Journey Round the World*, whose title page is shown here. *(Library of Congress, Prints and Photographs Division [LC-USZ62-108115])*

Photography in Africa

Soon after the invention of photography in 1839, explorers attempted to put this new technology to use. Within the same year, Sir John Herschel, an English astronomer, attempted to take photographs during a British expedition in the Antarctic. His efforts proved futile due to the cumbersome photographic apparatus, the fragile glass plates upon which the images were made, and, of course, the cold. Fortunately, explorers were not people to be easily discouraged. They took up new photographic technologies, such as the "wet plate" collodion process, invented by Frederick Scott Archer in 1851. This process produced higher-quality images but depended upon an awkward apparatus, glass plates, and the immediate application of chemicals. It is noteworthy that the exposure time for these early cameras could be as long as several minutes, during which subjects had to remain perfectly still in order to avoid blurring the image. Photography was not, in any of these respects, well suited to exploration in Africa. David Livingstone nevertheless brought the photographic team of Charles Livingstone and John Kirk on his Zambezi expedition. They, like the expedition as a whole, experienced numerous difficulties and disappointments in their work. Kirk succeeded in producing a number of landscape photographs, but it appears that Livingstone produced only one picture during the entire expedition.

In the 1870s, at the beginning of the so-called scramble for Africa, dry-plate photography was invented, replacing the wet-plate process that had necessitated immediate processing. The most important benefit of this new technology was that people could take photographs and then develop them at a later point in time, under controlled conditions. This is not to say that photography in Africa became easy. Arthur Conan Doyle, an amateur photographer and the creator of Sherlock Holmes, traveled to West Africa on a photographic expedition in the late 19th century. He experienced great frustration, due primarily to the heat and the humidity that weakened the seals of the bottles in which he stored his photographic chemicals. The particular problem of chemical reactions in the African climate would be resolved after 1888, when an American, George Eastman, introduced the box camera, called a Kodak. This camera captured images on a roll of paper, a transparent nitrocellulose coated with a gelatin emulsion, which the photographer, after returning to Europe, simply mailed to a Kodak lab for developing. In addition to sparing the photographer the need to develop his or her own pictures, the Kodak also featured a faster shutter speed that eliminated the need for a tripod. Finally, just as the creation of photographs was becoming more simple and reliable, their distribution was accelerated in the 1890s, when a new method for printing photos in half tones on high-speed presses made mass production in the press possible for the first time. This method enabled the general public in Europe, the United States, and elsewhere to see Africa through photographs in newspapers and magazines.

based not only on his explorations but also on the moral idealism that he had carried with him to Africa.

A SEAMAN TRAVELS OVERLAND

It seemed unlikely that a man who had made his living on the sea would be the first person to walk across equatorial Africa from east to west. Yet this was precisely what Verney Lovett Cameron did. Cameron joined the British Royal Navy in 1857 and served around the world, from the coast of India to the coast of Louisiana in the United States. He rose to the rank of lieutenant, and he was happy to be traveling so widely and often. Then, in the late 1860s, he was posted to a quiet port in England, where he quickly became bored. He dreamed of Africa, having been intrigued by accounts of the expeditions of Burton, Speke, and Livingstone. He also had his own experience of Africa. When serving aboard the HMS *Star* on the east coast of Africa, he had witnessed the cruelties of the slave trade. He explains in his memoir, *Across Africa*, "I soon became convinced that unless it could be attacked at its source in the interior of the continent all attempts at its suppression on the coast would be but a poor palliation of the fearful evil."

In 1870, while still stationed in England, Cameron attempted to persuade the Royal Geographical Society (RGS) to send him on an expedition to find Livingstone, who was presumed lost or dead. News that Henry Stanley had located Livingstone reached Britain before Cameron's expedition had been approved. Two years later, however, the RGS sent Cameron to provide support to Livingstone and then to undertake an independent exploration with Livingstone's assistance. Cameron and several British colleagues landed at Zanzibar in February 1873 and hired Speke and Stanley's former captain, Bombay, to lead the porters of their caravan. At the coastal town of Bagamoyo, they were joined by additional Europeans, including Robert Moffat, a Natal sugar planter who was Livingstone's nephew. They set off toward the Great Lakes region, where Livingstone was last reported, but were slowed by disease and the desertions of porters. Moffat died of fever, and Cameron and the remaining Europeans struggled with severe cases of fever as well. They were camped at Unyanyembe in the hope of recovering their health on October 20, when they received a letter from one of Livingstone's servants, indicating that Livingstone had died. They subsequently met Livingstone's servants, who were carrying Livingstone's remains to the coast. Part of Cameron's company chose to accompany the body, but Cameron and a naval surgeon, W. E. Dillon, were determined to push forward to Ujiji. A few weeks later, in a feverish delirium, Dillon shot himself and died, leaving Cameron with Bombay and the other Africans of the expedition. Cameron was having difficulty seeing, and he had recently suffered a back injury when he fell from a donkey, but he chose again to push forward. Upon arriving at Ujiji, he assembled Livingstone's remaining papers and sent them to the coast. He then explored and mapped much of the region around Ujiji, recording 96 rivers flowing into Lake Tanganyika and one flowing out of it. The latter river flowed into the Lukuga River and from there, Cameron was told, to the Lualaba. Most important, Cameron learned from merchants and slave traders at Ujiji that the Lualaba River probably flowed into the Congo. This information had certainly been given to Livingstone as well, but Livingstone had chosen to dismiss it. By contrast, Cameron listened closely to this advice and proceeded westward to follow the

Lualaba and discover whether it became the Nile or the Congo after all.

Cameron experienced more problems after leaving Ujiji, as when he entered the land of the Manyuema, who were reputed to be cannibals. Cameron explains: "They prepare the corpses by leaving them in running water until they are nearly putrid, and then devour them without any further cooking." Cameron's fears of being eaten were certainly greater than the actual threat. Like Livingstone before him, he found that his main difficulties lay in the demands of local chiefs for gifts and tribute in exchange for food or permission to pass through their territories. And like Livingstone, Cameron benefited from the assistance of slave traders. Recognizing that he needed both guidance and additional strength if he was going to survive this journey, Cameron joined a slave caravan, which brought him to the Lualaba in August 1874.

He marched downstream to Nyangwe, the same place where Livingstone had turned back from his quest for the source of the Nile in 1870. Cameron found that the merchants at Nyangwe would not provide him with canoes,

Hamed ibn Hamed, commonly known as Tippu Tip, was one of the most powerful slave traders in equatorial Africa. In this engraving, he sells some African people into bondage as Henry Morton Stanley observes. *(Library of Congress, Prints and Photographs Division [LC-USZ62-28351])*

and it appeared that his expedition might have no choice but to return eastward. He was then surprised one day to witness the arrival of the most powerful slave trader in equatorial Africa, Hamed ibn Hamed, more commonly known as Tippu Tip. Cameron found Tip to be keenly intelligent, cultured, and personable. Seeing Cameron's predicament, Tip advised the explorer to abandon the Lualaba River and proceed south, then west to Angola. Acting on Tip's advice, Cameron's expedition proceeded by itself and soon experienced conflicts with local tribes. In one incident, just beyond the Lukazi River, villagers stole Cameron's goat, named Dinah, which Cameron had brought along for a reliable supply of milk. Cameron insisted that the goat be returned, and in response the villagers attacked the expedition with arrows and spears. Cameron and his men returned fire with their guns and fled to the next village, where they were again greeted with a rain of arrows and spears. In desperation, Cameron and several of his men charged the village, firing their guns, and drove the inhabitants into the forest. Cameron then fortified the village, naming it Fort Dinah, in honor of his stolen goat. He and his men fought off their attackers for three days, inflicting casualties with their superior weaponry. Eventually, a settlement was reached and Cameron's expedition was permitted to carry on.

Cameron and his men subsequently entered the realm of King Kasongo, a brutal despot who was temporarily away from home in order to terrorize and steal from his subjects. Cameron was obliged to wait for the king's approval to proceed through the kingdom. In the meantime, he met a slave trader, José Antonio Alvez, who agreed to let Cameron's expedition join a large slave caravan that was due to return to Angola. In January 1875, Cameron finally met Kasongo, a tall young man. "After seeing me and my won-

ders," Cameron recalls, "he began begging for all I possessed—my own guns, hat, boots, pistols, books—in fact everything new to him he fancied and asked for . . ." At the same time that Cameron attempted to refuse, but not offend, the young king, he was troubled to see that Kasongo was accompanied by a large number of mutilated men. These men, who were missing ears, hands, and various other body parts, fawned over the king, singing his praises at every opportunity. Only later, Cameron was astonished to learn that these men had been mutilated by Kasongo himself. Cameron explains: "Under the combined influence of immoderate drinking and smoking of bhang [a narcotic], Kasongo acts like a demon, ordering death and mutilation indiscriminately and behaving in the most barbarous manner to any who may be near him."

Kasongo assured Cameron that he would someday visit England. Until then, Cameron's ruler was to pay him tribute, in the form of rifles, cannons, and boats. Cameron did his best to intimidate Kasongo with accounts of Queen Victoria's military power, and otherwise to humor the king and win his confidence. Above all, over the course of many weeks, Cameron attempted to persuade Kasongo to provide him with guides to take him north to the Congo River. Kasongo ignored these requests, and instead insisted that Cameron attend a royal function in which local chiefs would pay him tribute. Cameron was fortunate to learn ahead of time that Kasongo intended to use this function as a means to attack him and steal his belongings.

Kasongo initially asked Alvez to assist him in ambushing Cameron, but Alvez declined, perhaps because he planned to make a great deal of money from Cameron during their travel to Angola. Kasongo nonetheless found an ally in one of Alvez's subordinates, Lourenço da Souza Coimbra, whom Cameron describes as "a high grade ruffian." In anticipation of the royal function, Cameron posted 60 men around his camp and then took 60 more to meet Kasongo. The ceremony took place in a large enclosure, with Cameron's men on one side, facing their adversaries on the other. Kasongo sat pompously and received his local chiefs. Recognizing that Cameron was prepared to fight with superior weaponry, Kasongo decided to spare his guest, or himself, an ugly battle. Although he failed to kill Cameron, he succeeded in delaying his departure for several more months, during which he extracted more gifts and payments from the explorer. Cameron attempted to put his idle time to use. As he explains: "Many otherwise tedious hours were occupied in writing, drawing . . . and in copying itineraries and meteorological observations for my journals."

The caravan finally departed in June 1875 with more than 1,500 slaves. "The conduct of Alvez's men on the road was disgraceful," commented Cameron. "They attacked any small parties of natives whom they chanced to meet and plundered their loads, though these consisted chiefly of dried fish and corn which were being carried as tribute to Kasongo." As a result of the slave traders' actions, the caravan found virtually every village along its path empty of people and livestock. Another result was that the caravan was under constant threat of attack. Cameron observes that they were careful in passing through the jungle, "for it was reported to be full of armed men who would cut off stragglers, and, according to rumour, kill and eat them."

The caravan descended into a region of swamps. They waded through mud that was waist-deep and across fallen trees, where a misstep left one submerged in stagnant water and rotting vegetation. At one point Cameron found himself among anthills 40 to 50 feet in height. "It is as though a nation had set to work and built Mount Everest," he remarked in his journal. In July 1875, having passed through the swamps, Cameron was horrified to see Coimbra emerge from the forest with 52 women tied together, many carrying children. Cameron, the same man who had been inspired to explore Africa in order to combat slavery, found that his life now depended on slave traders such as Coimbra. Moreover, he realized that his men had no confidence in his leadership and would desert him if he left the caravan. So, with 52 additional slave women, Cameron marched forward.

The going became more difficult, and the slave traders exacted increasingly larger payments from Cameron for guidance and food. When the caravan reached Angola, the slave traders stopped at their base and left Cameron and his men to continue on their own to the coast. As the expedition approached Bihé, Cameron had to sell his own shirts to feed his men. Further on, they were reduced to eating locusts. Suffering from scurvy, Cameron struggled into the Portuguese station at Katombela on November 7, 1875, where a Portuguese official greeted him in disbelief, then opened a bottle of wine to celebrate the first European to traverse Africa from east to west. Cameron was in no condition to celebrate, try as he might. He was carried to Benguela, on the coast, where a European surgeon saved his life.

Cameron returned to Liverpool in April 1876 and was hailed as the greatest explorer since Livingstone. He was promoted to the rank of commander in the Royal Navy, and he received gold medals from the Royal Geographical Society and the Geographical Society of Paris, and a special medal from King Victor Emmanuel of Italy, among many other rewards. In a lecture tour of Britain, he extolled the commercial potential of Africa,

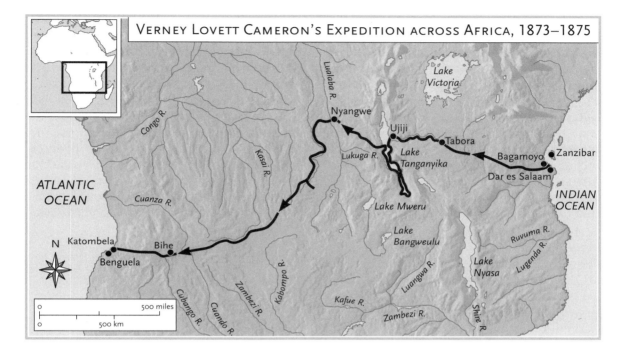

VERNEY LOVETT CAMERON'S EXPEDITION ACROSS AFRICA, 1873–1875

emphasizing plantation products such as cotton, coffee, and tobacco. He had also seen an abundance of copper in the Katanga region, and he reported that Africa might hold great mineral wealth—not only in copper but also in gold, silver, and coal. Cameron believed that the successful development of Africa depended on the dual progress of commerce and Christianity. In *Across Africa* he observes, "Commercial enterprise and missionary effort, instead of acting in opposition, as is too often the case, should do their best to assist each other." Cameron would subsequently lead expeditions into the Middle East, seeking a secure overland trade route to Asia, and then—with Richard Burton—to West Africa in search of gold mines. In the 1880s he retired from the navy and turned his energies to commercial interests in Africa. In March 1894 he was thrown from a horse and killed.

THE LUALABA BECOMES THE CONGO

Cameron's belief that the Lualaba flowed into the Congo River would soon be tested by Henry Stanley. Stanley had already achieved fame by finding Livingstone in 1871, but geographers had declined to pay him respect as an explorer. They regarded Stanley as merely a publicity monger, frustrating his intense personal desire for respect and approval. He had been awed and inspired by Livingstone, who was commonly regarded as the greatest explorer of his era. Consequently, when Stanley learned in 1873 that Livingstone had died, he decided to carry on Livingstone's work by resolving one of the most pressing geographical questions of the day: Was the Lualaba the source of the Nile or the Congo? And if it was the source of the Congo, was it possible to navigate down the river to the west coast, thus providing a highway into the center of the continent?

Stanley obtained funding for his expedition from the New York *Herald* and London's *Daily Telegraph,* which would have exclusive rights to his reports of his travels. Stanley returned to Africa in 1874 and gathered together his caravan at Bagamoyo. In November he marched inland at the head of a column of 359 people, including three European companions and African women and children. Their progress was difficult from the outset. Within just two months, in January 1875, 20 had died, 89 had

deserted, and many were sick. Stanley nonetheless reached Lake Victoria, where he assembled a portable boat, the *Lady Alice,* that he had brought from England. In this boat he became the first European to circumnavigate both Lake Victoria and, subsequently, Lake Tanganyika. He observes of Lake Victoria: "Oh for the hour when a band of philanthropic capitalists shall vow to rescue these beautiful lands, and supply the means to enable the Gospel messengers to come and quench the murderous hate with which man beholds man in the beautiful lands around Lake Victoria!"

A Portable Boat

In anticipation of his second major expedition in Africa, Stanley ordered the construction of a portable boat. He intended to use this boat to circumnavigate both Lake Victoria and Lake Tanganyika, and then to travel down the Congo River to the sea. Having led a previous expedition in Africa, he was aware of the difficulties that one might encounter in obtaining transportation, and he further desired to have a boat more sturdy than the canoes he might purchase. Verney Lovett Cameron had already envisioned a European vessel on the upper Congo River, but Stanley was the first to put this vision into practice. He ordered the boat to be built by James Messenger, a boatbuilder in Teddington, near London. Stanley observed in *Through the Dark Continent:* "It was to be 40 feet long, 6 feet beam, and 30 inches deep, of Spanish cedar 3/8 inch thick. When finished, it was to be separated into five sections, each of which should be 8 feet long. If the sections should be over-weight, they were to be again divided into halves for greater facility of carriage." Before departure into the interior, Stanley had the boat modified into eight sections, three feet wide. He hired a set of particularly large and strong men to carry the sections of the boat, and he acknowledged the special status of these porters by allowing them to bring their wives. Once on the Congo, Stanley's portable boat served the expedition well. Moreover, the boat proved to be an asset in Stanley's eight pitched battles on the river. Stanley had named the boat the *Lady Alice,* after Miss Alice Pike of New York. He was engaged to marry Pike when he departed on his expedition in 1874, but she married another man before his return. The boat proved to be far more reliable than the woman after which it was named. Stanley regretted having to abandon the vessel at the final, impassible cataracts that separated the upper and lower Congo.

For his second expedition in Africa, Henry Stanley had a portable boat, which he named *Lady Alice*, constructed. He and his party had to carry the pieces of this boat with their canoes and supplies through the dense jungles lining the bank of the Lualaba River. This lithograph shows what this process might have looked like. *(Library of Congress, Prints and Photographs Division [LC-USZC4-3225])*

Stanley confirmed Cameron's finding that Lake Tanganyika did not empty into the Nile but into the Lukuga River. Stanley then followed Livingstone and Cameron to Nyangwe, where both men had failed to secure passage down the river. Again, Tippu Tip was at Nyangwe, and he and Stanley soon found themselves on friendly terms. Stanley succeeded in purchasing the support of the slave trader, who accompanied him in a march down the river with 1,000 men. The jungle along the river was so dense that Stanley was sometimes reduced to crawling on his hands and knees, while the porters, and particularly the men carrying the sections of the *Lady Alice*, labored under tortuous conditions. To make matters worse, the expedition was regularly attacked by local peoples, who had the advantage of knowing the terrain. After about 200 miles, Tip refused to go any farther and turned back, leaving Stanley and his people to proceed on the river in the *Lady Alice* and 22 canoes they had acquired both by purchase and combat since leaving Nyangwe.

Stanley's exploration of the river proved to be an epic, often horrifying experience. He and his followers fought almost three dozen battles on land and on the river. Stanley

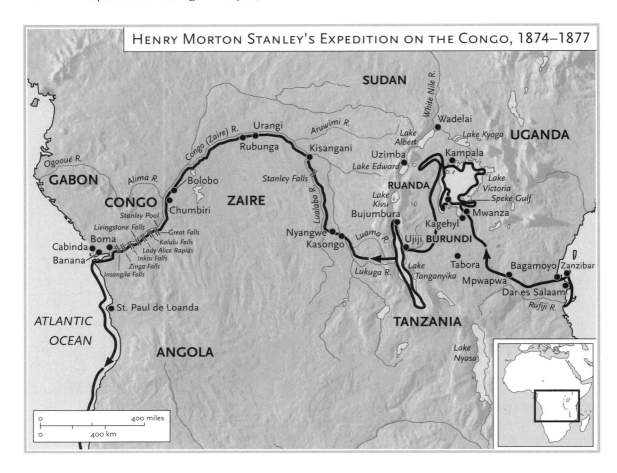

HENRY MORTON STANLEY'S EXPEDITION ON THE CONGO, 1874–1877

gained a reputation for brutality, but, if one carefully reads his account of his travels, one finds that he avoided far more fights than he engaged. Stanley understood that this was not a military expedition.

> It was an expedition organized solely for the purposes of exploration, with a view to search out new avenues of commerce to the mutual advantage of civilization and such strange lands as we found suitable for commercial and missionary enterprise. But whatever its character, its members possessed the privilege of self-defence.

Stanley's greatest adversaries were undoubtedly the river, disease, and hunger, that "gaunt monster," in Stanley's words. The expedition struggled constantly against malaria, typhoid, and dysentery, and the river confronted them with impassable waterfalls and cataracts. Separating the upper and lower river is a series of 32 cataracts, covering approximately 220 miles, where the last of Stanley's European companions, Frank Pocock, drowned. Stanley had to leave the *Lady Alice* along these cataracts and walk the remainder of the distance to the sea. Having determined that the Lualaba flowed into the

King Leopold II of Belgium

King Leopold II had visions of glory that might have been suitable for a European great power such as Great Britain, France, or Germany. Unfortunately for Leopold, he was the monarch of Belgium, a small country that was unable to stand up to its neighbor, France, without guarantees of protection from Britain. Yet Leopold was an ambitious and brilliant man who would not be deterred from enhancing Belgium's status in Europe. He intended to do this by acquiring an overseas empire. He began looking for a foreign region to which he might lay claim, but this was no easy task, given that he was entering the business of empire relatively late. He surveyed East and Southeast Asia without success, but then in 1875 his attention was drawn to equatorial Africa by Verney Lovett Cameron's successful expedition across the continent. Leopold was particularly interested in Cameron's accounts of the resources and riches to be found in Africa.

In 1876, Leopold established the International African Association, an organization that would encourage further exploration and scientific investigation in tropical Africa. In fact, this association was a front for Leopold's own imperial plans. After Henry Stanley tracked the length of the Congo in 1877, Leopold moved quickly to hire him to return to the Congo on his behalf. On the strength of his support for European exploration on the Congo, Leopold then used the Berlin Conference of 1884–85 as his opportunity to lay claim to the region. He knew that while the great

(continues)

Leopold II, king of Belgium from 1865 until his death in 1909, established the Congo Free State in 1885 and ruled it until accusations of mistreatment forced him to cede the colony to the Belgian nation in 1908. *(Library of Congress, Prints and Photographs Division [LC-USZ62-130449])*

(continued)

powers at the conference wanted to profit from the Congo, they did not want to bear the costs of imperial administration in this vast region. At the same time, each power did not want another power to take control of the Congo. So Leopold promised everyone that the African Association would establish an administration over the Congo that would open the region to all European merchants and missionaries. The European powers agreed and granted the association control over the Congo. Just five months after the Berlin Conference ended in 1885, Leopold unilaterally declared his *personal* sovereignty over the Congo, which became known as the Congo Free State. Leopold made a fortune from the Congo, but news of the brutality of the Congo Free State provoked a scandal in Europe in the early part of the 20th century. Leopold ceded control over the Congo to the Belgian nation in 1908, only after the profitability of the Congo had substantially decreased.

Congo River, Stanley miraculously descended to the European outpost at Boma, about 110 miles from the coast, in August 1877. Of the 359 people who set off with Stanley in 1874, only 82 returned. Stanley chronicled his exploration in *Through the Dark Continent,* which became an international best-seller upon its publication in 1878. Stanley's critics among the armchair geographers would continue to fault his brutal methods, but no one would again question his status as one of the greatest explorers of the 19th century.

Upon Stanley's return to Europe, he was approached by King Leopold II of Belgium, who had become interested in the commercial prospects of central Africa after Cameron's transcontinental journey. Stanley agreed to work on behalf of the king and so traveled back to the Congo in 1878. As Leopold's employee, Stanley worked for the next five years to secure the south bank of the Congo River by negotiation and force, building stations and trading networks, both by order and by example. He received the nick-

name Bula Matari ("breaker of rocks") from African laborers who watched him swing a hammer in road construction. Stanley left King Leopold's service in 1884, having laid the foundation of the Congo Free State, which Leopold established in the following year.

RACING FOR THE POOL

Stanley had a remarkable competitor on the Congo: Count Pietro di Brazza Savorgnani, born an Italian aristocrat and self-made as a French explorer. As a child growing up near Rome, Brazza had become fascinated by overseas travel and exploration. Given that Italy did not have a strong navy, Brazza enrolled at the age of 18 in the French naval academy at Brest in 1870. Three years later he adopted French citizenship and changed his name to Pierre Savorgnan de Brazza. With the help of his family's aristocratic connections, he persuaded the French government to back him in leading a series of expeditions into central Africa from the coast of Gabon. Inspired by Livingstone's methods of exploration, he decided early in his travels that he would get farther by patient negotiation with Africans than by attempting to overpower those who stood in his way. Brazza was, of necessity, prepared to fight, but he preferred what was called a palaver. Two parties, or sometimes multiple parties, engaged in a palaver by sitting down—generally surrounded by their respective people—and settling issues through explanation, the exchange of goods, and expressions of trust. As a master of the palaver, Brazza gained a reputation as a man of peace, and he thus succeeded in building long-standing, cooperative relationships with many of the tribes whose lands he visited.

In 1875, accompanied by Senegalese sailors provided to him by the French navy, Brazza landed at the mouth of the Gabon River and hired dozens of boatmen and porters at Lambaréné. He then traveled into the interior, investigating prospects for commerce and colonization while trading cloth, glassware, and tools. He also encountered some previously unmapped rivers. He was particularly interested in exploring the Ogowe River, hoping that its source would lay somewhere in the center of the continent. In 1877 he found that the Ogowe began to diminish several hundred miles inland, so he turned down the Alima River, beyond which, according to the local people, ran the "big water." To Brazza's surprise, the Apfourus tribe attacked him on the Alima, despite his efforts to have a palaver. He and his men were forced to leave their canoes, much of their baggage, and flee for their lives to higher ground. Unbeknownst to Brazza, he and Henry Stanley were proceeding into the same region of central Africa at approximately the same time from the west and the east. Only after his return to Europe in 1878 did Brazza learn that the Alima emptied into the Congo, and that Stanley had passed through the area some months before him. Brazza declared that Stanley's violent methods of exploration had incited the local people to attack white men.

The French government sponsored Brazza in another expedition between 1879 and 1882, with a view toward establishing a foothold for French commerce in central Africa. Brazza was officially embarking on a geographical expedition under the auspices of the Paris Geographical Society, but he had two secret missions for the government as well. First, Brazza was to establish a station that would connect the Ogowe and the upper Congo Rivers. Second, he was to reach Stanley Pool, a body of water just above the cataracts and at the entrance to the navigable upper river, and claim it for the French. Remarkably, King Leopold II of Belgium had just hired Stanley to return up the Congo, establish a series of stations, and secure Stanley Pool for him. Of course, Stanley felt a certain sense of ownership for the pool, having given it his own name when he found it in 1877. Suspecting that the French had their own designs on the Congo, Stanley departed quietly from Europe under an assumed name at almost the same time that Brazza set off with similar objects in mind. It was a race for Stanley Pool.

Stanley clearly had the more difficult route to the pool because he had to build a series of stations and roads along the Congo as he advanced. Brazza retraced his path up the Ogowe and then marched overland, bypassing the cataracts on the Congo to reach Stanley Pool ahead of Stanley. In the process, Brazza discovered that there was almost no water to be found between the upper Ogowe and the upper Congo, a discovery that nearly killed him. When he finally reached the Congo, he threw himself into drink, then celebrated by falling asleep.

Brazza presented himself to the strongest chief in the region of Stanley Pool, King

Makoko. Brazza dressed up for the occasion, wearing his blue naval uniform, with his Senegalese men behind him in their sailor suits. He succeeded in signing a treaty with the king, on the basis of which the French would declare a protectorate over Makoko's kingdom. This treaty, among others, enabled the French to claim the north shore of the lower Congo River and establish a station on the pool, which came to be called Brazzaville. Brazza also held a palaver with the lesser chiefs in the region, the Abanhos, employing a friendly and generous manner that was typical of his negotiating tactics by this time. He held in his right hand rifle cartridges, and in his left hand he held cloth. He said, "White men have two hands. The stronger hand is the hand of war. The other hand is the hand of trade. Which hand do Abanhos want?" "Trade," the chiefs declared. Brazza then threw the cartridges into a hole and planted a tree on top of them. "May there never be war again," he declared, "until this tree bears a crop of cartridges." With his treaty in hand, Brazza left the Senegalese to man a station that they had built on the north shore of the pool, he told Makoko not to trade with any other Europeans, and he then returned to the coast. Makoko and the lesser chiefs would subsequently follow Brazza's orders. As Stanley made his way up the Congo, he encountered two members of the Baptist Missionary Society who had reached the pool and then fled, because the local chiefs threatened to kill them.

The French government ratified Brazza's treaty with Makoko in November 1882. In 1886, Brazza was appointed governor-general of the French Congo, and he worked in this post for the next 12 years. He was known for his insistence on the fair and humane treatment of Africans, and he built a number of schools and health clinics. Brazza was later sent back by the French government to investigate alleged abuses by colonial officials in the early 20th century. Brazza wrote a critical report and then died on his way home, at Dakar, Senegal, in 1905. Brazzaville, the capital of the Republic of Congo, remains one of the only cities in Africa to retain the name of its imperial founder.

UNDERSTANDING AFRICAN CULTURE AND COMMERCE

Mary Kingsley first set out for West Africa in 1893 in search of "beetles, fishes, and fetish." She was a member of an English family of distinguished intellectuals. As the author of *West African Studies,* she was regarded as a leading figure in the study of West African culture during the high era of imperialism. She advocated the principle of cultural relativism, which recognized that each culture has its own integrity and must be understood in its own terms. Kingsley argued through publications and lectures that Europe's perception of African savagery displayed Europe's own inability to understand Africans. Africans, Kingsley asserted, were different from Europeans and should not be compelled to conform to European social customs, moral standards, and industrial economy.

Kingsley took a dim view of missionaries and religious conversion, a view that was commonly shared by merchants and imperial officials. She advocated tolerance of polygamy —the practice of having marital and sexual relations with multiple partners—and other aspects of African culture that missionaries abhorred. Kingsley mocked missionaries in Africa who ". . . wrote their reports not to tell you how the country they resided in was, but how it was getting on towards being what it ought to be. . . ." Time and again, Kingsley asserted that missionary "civilization" caused African "degeneration" by undermining the traditional order of African society. In contrast to missionaries, Kingsley asserted, merchants promoted the constructive development of African societies. Kingsley was a strong proponent of the importance of commercial relations and free trade between Africans and Europeans.

Kingsley preferred commerce to "commerce and Christianity," but she did not advocate commerce between equals. She asserted that the difference between Africans and Europeans was not ". . . a difference of degree but of kind," and she believed that this difference in kind was reflected in "a large number of anatomical facts" and a far larger number of what she called "mental attributes." ". . . I feel certain," Kingsley stated, "that . . . the mental difference between the two races is very similar to that between men and women among ourselves. A great woman, either mentally or physically, will excel an indifferent man, but no woman ever equals a really great man." Kingsley believed that the African mind was acute but lacked discipline; that Africans were prone to sloth, and that they were deficient in the mechanical arts. She wrote:

> . . . They have never made, unless under white direction and instruction, a single fourteenth-rate piece of cloth, pottery, a tool or machine, house, road, bridge, picture or statue. . . .

Kingsley took a relatively positive view toward African culture in comparison with other Europeans of her era, but she nonetheless displayed some biases that were typical of her time. Moreover, she did not actually have wide experiences in African cultures, which is perhaps why she overlooked the beautiful bronzeworks of Benin, in west Africa, and other examples of Africans' artistic accomplishments.

She believed that, through commercial relations with Europeans, Africans would develop discipline of mind and mechanical skills that would enhance their welfare in their societies. In Kingsley's opinion, commerce between unequal peoples could be mutually beneficial, provided that each party respected the other's differences. Although she was not solely responsible for spreading the idea of cultural relativism, she did exert considerable personal influence over a number of future political leaders and humanitarian activists. Kingsley died as a volunteer nurse during the South African War in 1900.

The European exploration of central Africa had almost immediate consequences for many of the peoples of the region, and especially those in the Congo River basin. Within just a year of his successful exploration of the Congo, Stanley was hired to return up the river to lay the foundation for a European imperial regime, the Congo Free State. While Stanley, Brazza, and the other major explorers had justified their work as a campaign against the African slave trade, the empires that they helped to create then exploited and coerced Africans through what humanitarian critics would call "new systems of slavery." Local African rulers, such as those who signed treaties with Stanley and Brazza, would participate in and profit from this exploitation, thus dividing Africans against themselves in the face of European expansion. In the middle of the 19th century, the European map of Africa had been largely blank, except for the coastal regions and the Muslim countries to the North. By the early 20th century, it would be filled by the paths of rivers, which European merchants, missionaries, and generals had followed to lay the boundaries of their empires in the wake of the great explorers.

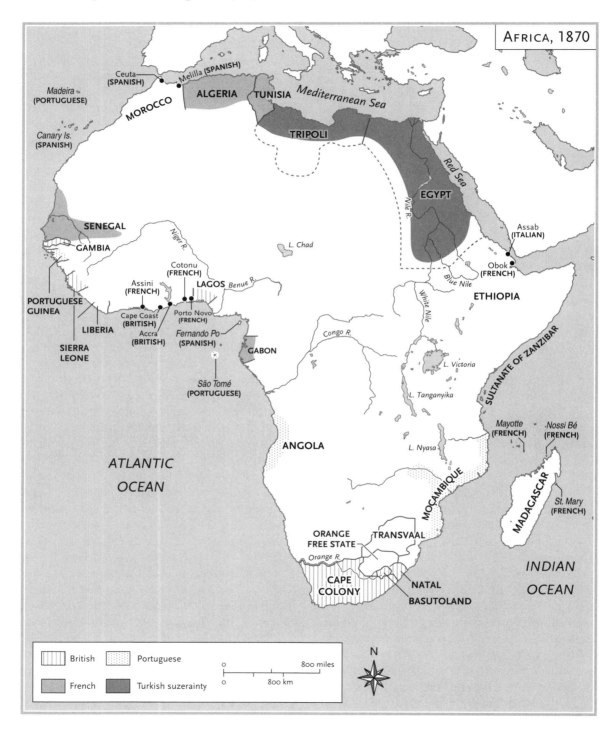

AFRICA, 1870

Ceuta (SPANISH)
Melilla (SPANISH)
Madeira (PORTUGUESE)
MOROCCO
ALGERIA
TUNISIA
Mediterranean Sea
TRIPOLI
Canary Is. (SPANISH)
Red Sea
EGYPT
Nile R.
Assab (ITALIAN)
SENEGAL
Niger R.
L. Chad
Obok (FRENCH)
GAMBIA
Blue Nile
ETHIOPIA
PORTUGUESE GUINEA
Cotonu (FRENCH)
Assini (FRENCH)
LAGOS
Benue R.
White Nile
LIBERIA
Cape Coast (BRITISH)
Porto Novo (FRENCH)
SIERRA LEONE
Accra (BRITISH)
Fernando Po (SPANISH)
Congo R.
SULTANATE OF ZANZIBAR
GABON
São Tomé (PORTUGUESE)
L. Victoria
L. Tanganyika
Mayotte (FRENCH)
Nossi Bé (FRENCH)
ATLANTIC OCEAN
ANGOLA
L. Nyasa
MADAGASCAR
St. Mary (FRENCH)
MOÇAMBIQUE
ORANGE FREE STATE
TRANSVAAL
INDIAN OCEAN
Orange R.
CAPE COLONY
NATAL
BASUTOLAND

British
Portuguese
French
Turkish suzerainty

0   800 miles
0   800 km

N

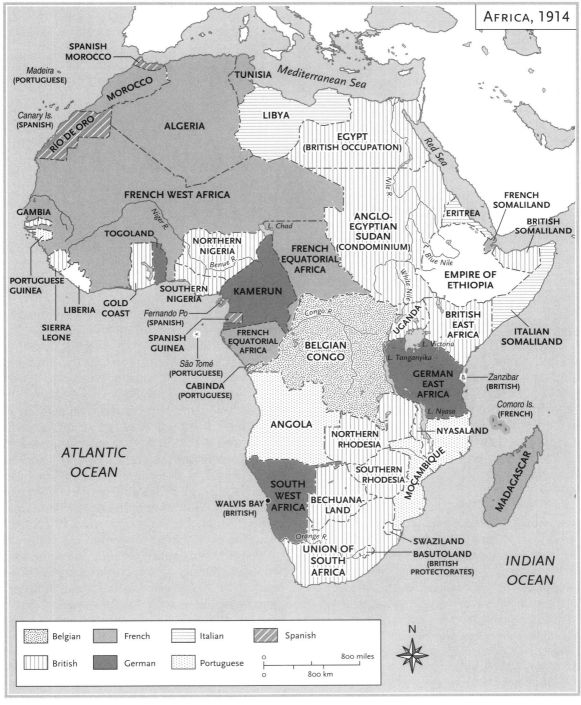

AFRICA, 1914

SPANISH MOROCCO

Madeira (PORTUGUESE)

Canary Is. (SPANISH)

TUNISIA

Mediterranean Sea

RIO DE ORO

MOROCCO

ALGERIA

LIBYA

EGYPT (BRITISH OCCUPATION)

Red Sea

Nile R.

FRENCH WEST AFRICA

GAMBIA

Niger R.

TOGOLAND

NORTHERN NIGERIA

Benue R.

L. Chad

FRENCH EQUATORIAL AFRICA

ANGLO-EGYPTIAN SUDAN (CONDOMINIUM)

Blue Nile

ERITREA

FRENCH SOMALILAND

BRITISH SOMALILAND

PORTUGUESE GUINEA

LIBERIA

GOLD COAST

SOUTHERN NIGERIA

Fernando Po (SPANISH)

SPANISH GUINEA

KAMERUN

White Nile

EMPIRE OF ETHIOPIA

SIERRA LEONE

FRENCH EQUATORIAL AFRICA

Congo R.

BELGIAN CONGO

UGANDA

L. Victoria

BRITISH EAST AFRICA

ITALIAN SOMALILAND

São Tomé (PORTUGUESE)

CABINDA (PORTUGUESE)

L. Tanganyika

GERMAN EAST AFRICA

Zanzibar (BRITISH)

Comoro Is. (FRENCH)

ANGOLA

L. Nyasa

NYASALAND

NORTHERN RHODESIA

MOÇAMBIQUE

ATLANTIC OCEAN

SOUTHERN RHODESIA

MADAGASCAR

SOUTH WEST AFRICA

WALVIS BAY (BRITISH)

BECHUANA-LAND

Orange R.

SWAZILAND

UNION OF SOUTH AFRICA

BASUTOLAND (BRITISH PROTECTORATES)

INDIAN OCEAN

Belgian French Italian Spanish

British German Portuguese

0   800 miles
0   800 km

N

6

PILGRIMAGES TO MECCA AND THE ARABIAN SANDS

Harry St. John Bridger Philby was marching toward disappointment in the Rub' al-Khali, the Empty Quarter, of the Arabian Peninsula in 1932. The Empty Quarter was a large inland desert in the southern half of the peninsula, one of the few places on earth still unknown to geographers. Philby was attempting to explore and survey the region, but he was confronting both a brutal landscape and growing discontent among his Arab followers. He wrote in *Saudi Arabia* (1955):

> Drought and famine stalked the land with drawn swords of flaming fire, breathing hotly upon us who ventured thus into their domain. It was impressive but it was depressing, and I was oppressed, maybe, by a premonition of failure. Grimly and in silence we marched on over an endless succession of valleys and ridges, hoping that each crest would gladden our eyes with a vision of pastures ahead, but hoping in vain.

He had been waiting for years to undertake this expedition, and he had finally secured the approval and support of the head of the Saudi royal family, Ibn Sa'ud. Now, just five days and 140 miles into their journey, Philby's men had lost their nerve. Had Philby wished only to speed their camel caravan across the desert in the cool of the night, the men would not have been troubled. But Philby saw no point in merely traversing the Empty Quarter. This had been recently done for the first time, to Philby's chagrin, by another explorer, Bertram Thomas. As Philby could not be the first European through the Empty Quarter, he now proposed to be the most thorough. He proposed to travel by day along a circuitous route and conduct a meticulous survey of the landscape under the blazing sun. His guides and servants saw no reason in this. There was no prospect of commerce or settlement in this desolate region. There was no prospect of mass religious conversion, given that there were few residents of the Empty Quarter and, moreover, that Philby himself had already converted to Islam. Actually, Philby's reason for undertaking this expedition was both simple and self-serving: He wished to achieve fame. He attempted to rally his men but to no avail. He accompanied the expedition back to their point of departure and then, famously, returned to survey the Empty Quarter with great success throughout the remainder of his life.

Philby was the most influential European explorer of the Arabian Peninsula, and, like many others before him, he came to his explorations through the expansion and competition of European empires. As an officer in the Indian Expeditionary Force to Mesopotamia during World War I, Philby was sent on a diplomatic mission to one of the most powerful Arab leaders on the peninsula, Ibn Sa'ud, the king of Saudi Arabia, in 1917. Somewhere along the camel ride to central Arabia and back, Philby had found his calling as an explorer and, in Ibn Sa'ud, his patron. In some important respects, Philby was typical of the great European explorers of the Arabian Peninsula in the modern era. He was tough, determined, and brave. He was also an aggressive individualist, taking his own path through and around conventional institutions. Finally, he was typical of most in his respect for Islam and his appreciation of Arabic culture.

The Arabian Peninsula is located in the southwestern corner of Asia, comprising an area of about 1 million square miles. To the west, the Red Sea separates the peninsula from northeast Africa. The peninsula is then surrounded by the Arabian Sea to the south, and the Sea of Oman and the Persian Gulf to the northeast. The southern and eastern coastlines are occupied by Muslim states, including Yemen. In the 18th and 19th centuries, the northern boundary of the peninsula was marked by Palestine (now Israel and the Palestinian Territories), Syria, Persia (now

Ibn Sa'ud founded Saudi Arabia in 1932 by consolidating various territories on the Arabian Peninsula. *(National Archives, Franklin D. Roosevelt Library, NLR-PHOCO-A-491642008[256])*

Iraq), and Kuwait. The remainder of the peninsula—and by far its largest part—was then roughly divided between two areas. The Hejaz, the fertile region on the west coast, held the Muslim holy sites of Mecca and Medina and had long been active in the trade networks between Africa and Asia. East of the Hejaz was the Najd, the large, arid region of central Arabia that was bordered by the Nafúd Desert to the north and the Empty Quarter, the largest desert on the peninsula, to the south. The Najd, like the Hejaz, was populated by Arab peoples who increasingly settled in towns and cities, but it also included the

Bedouin peoples, migratory tribes that defied central government authority. The Najd had been historically isolated from the dynamic cultural and economic developments in the Hejaz, and in the early 19th century it remained virtually unknown to Europeans.

European overseas exploration had begun during an era of intense rivalry between Christendom and Islam. As the modern era of exploration began in the 18th century, the balance of power in this rivalry was shifting in favor of Europe's Christian powers. By the mid-19th century, the British usurped the power of the Mughal emperor in South Asia, and the Russians conquered most of the khanates and emirates in Central Asia. In eastern Europe and the Middle East, the Ottoman Empire, with its center of power in present-day Turkey, was threatened by the growing industries and modern militaries of both western Europe and Russia. Most of the Arabian Peninsula was subject to the Ottoman ruler, who held the dual position of sultan and caliph. The first title defined his political authority, and the second designated his spiritual authority as the leader of Muslims around the world. It was crucially important that the Ottoman ruler maintain his control over the Muslim holy sites, and especially Mecca and Medina, located in western Arabia.

The Ottoman Empire was threatened on the Arabian Peninsula, not only by European powers but also by the Arabs themselves. In the 18th century, a fundamentalist movement for religious reform, known as the Wahhabi movement, gathered strength in central Arabia and allied itself with the Sa'udi dynasty, which then declared a new state in defiance of the Ottoman Empire. In 1802, Prince Sa'ud I captured Mecca, and in 1804 he captured Medina, asserting Wahhabi authority over most of the peninsula. The Ottoman sultan responded by appointing a new ruler in Egypt, Muhammad 'Ali Pasha, whose forces reoccupied Mecca and Medina in 1812. The Wahhabi uprising was put down in 1815, but, after the beheadings and exiles of various rebel leaders and their families, the movement rose again in the Najd to declare an independent state, with its capital at Riyadh, in 1824. During the remainder of the century, the fortunes of the Sa'udi dynasty would no longer be threatened by the Ottomans but by dissenting factions within the Wahhabi movement and by Arab rivals, especially the Rashidi. The Wahhabi movement again collapsed in 1891, only to be restored to power by Ibn Sa'ud, the future patron of Philby, in 1902. In short, from the 18th century until the 1930s, the European exploration of the Arabian Peninsula took place in the midst of violent political turmoil.

ENLIGHTENED EXPLORATIONS IN ARABIA

Until the 19th century, Europeans' interest in the Arabian Peninsula extended no farther than its coasts. The British and the Dutch had regular trade relations with Yemen in the south, and European merchants traveled or resided more than 100 miles inland to purchase Yemen's famous coffee. Yet most of the Arabian Peninsula, from the southern edge of the Empty Quarter to the northern edge of the desert of Nafúd, remained unvalued and, therefore, unexplored by Europeans. In the era of the Enlightenment, there were certainly those who took a scientific interest in the interior regions of Arabia, but they were generally discouraged by reports of unforgiving desert terrain, terrible heat, and the Bedouin, whom they considered savage peoples. Many Europeans had heard of Mecca and Medina, cities sacred to Islam, but the few Europeans who had visited these places were almost all converts to Islam and indifferent to exploration.

The Arabian Peninsula eventually became the object of scientific inquiry, thanks to the patronage of Frederik V, the king of Denmark, in the late 1750s. He agreed to sponsor an international scientific expedition to Yemen, the most familiar part of Arabia at that time. This expedition was led by Carsten Niebuhr, a German engineer and surveyor. He was accompanied by an artist, a botanist, a zoologist, an orientalist scholar, and a former soldier, who acted as a servant. In 1760 the expedition sailed from Copenhagen in Denmark to Egypt, where it remained for one year as its members improved their Arabic and made additional preparations for their journey to Yemen. They then proceeded aboard a boat loaded with pilgrims to the port city of Jidda, and from there to the port of Loheia in Yemen. After four months on the coast, they traveled inland on donkeys, passing through an arid landscape scattered with villages and coffee shops, where they stopped regularly for refreshment. Although they did not attempt to conceal their identities as Europeans, the men attempted to conform as best they could to the culture of the Yemeni people. Toward this end, Niebuhr traveled in Yemeni attire, with a saber and two pistols in his belt, and a bucket of water hanging from the piece of carpet that was his saddle. They reached the town of Beit el-Fakih, a central coffee market, and decided to make this their base of operations. From here they visited the neighboring foothills and fertile valleys, admiring the many coffee plantations that were the basis of the regional economy.

They proceeded eastward into the mountains, which rose to heights of 8,000 feet. Niebuhr observed in his *Description of Arabia*, "The hills are to be climbed by steep and narrow paths; yet, in comparison with the parched plains . . . the scenery seemed to me charming, as it was covered with gardens and plantations of coffee trees." The members of the expedition often found themselves traveling upon well-maintained roads, some of which were paved, and they enjoyed the hospitality of the many villages in the area. Unfortunately, despite the beauty and security of their journeys, a couple of members of the expedition died of disease during these travels in the mountains.

After several months the expedition proceeded northward to Sana, the capital of Yemen, this time assuming Arab names and the appearance of Arab Christians. They found Sana situated at the foot of a mountain and dominated by a citadel. The city was small enough to walk around in just one day, and it featured several impressive mosques and many palaces built of burnt bricks and cut stones. Beyond the city walls was a beautiful garden and, beyond, a fertile region where one found many kinds of fruit, including 12 varieties of grapes. Niebuhr and his colleagues were graciously received by the ruler of Yemen, the imam, al-Mahdi 'Abbas bin al-Mansur Husain, who gave them money, new clothes, and camels. Desiring not to overstay their welcome, the Europeans left Sana after less than a week and made their departure from Yemen aboard an English merchant ship bound for Bombay. As they crossed the Indian Ocean, the remainder of Niebuhr's European companions died. Niebuhr nonetheless reached India, sent home his journals from Yemen, and traveled back to Europe through Persia, Armenia, and Asia Minor, arriving in Denmark in 1767. He subsequently published his *Description of Arabia* in German in 1772, enhancing Europeans' appreciation of Arabic culture and the Arab peoples.

Although Niebuhr did not extend Europe's geographical knowledge of the Arabian

Peninsula, he enabled later explorers to approach the Arab people in a different light. Prior to Niebuhr's *Description,* Europeans commonly regarded Arabs either as dangerous infidels or as thieving savages. By contrast, Niebuhr offered a balanced portrait of Arabs as a noble and hospitable people with a complex culture. Most important, he rejected the common European belief that Muslims were naturally bent upon the destruction of Christianity. On the contrary, he assured Europe's Christians that Muslims generally did not persecute people of other religions unless those people gave them something to fear.

TO MECCA

While European merchants focused primarily on the southern Arabian Peninsula, European imperial governments also focused on Mecca, which they understood to be the center of Muslim power. Every year, millions of Muslims undertook the hajj, the pilgrimage to Mecca that each Muslim is to complete at least once in his or her lifetime. Europeans also went on the hajj, whether as Muslim converts or as agents of imperial masters. Six years after Napoleon Bonaparte invaded Egypt in 1798, he dispatched a Spaniard, Domingo Badía y Leblic, on the hajj to Mecca

Mecca ⁓

Mecca is the holiest city of the Islamic faith. Muslims pray five times a day in the direction of Mecca, and every Muslim hopes to complete the pilgrimage to Mecca, called the hajj, at least once in his or her lifetime. Before the rise of the Islamic faith in the seventh century, Mecca was an important city along the ancient caravan route that connected East Africa, the Arabian Peninsula, and South Asia. The city gained its religious status through its association with the prophet Muhammad, who was born in Mecca in 570 and lived there until 622, when he was forced to flee. In a cave located outside the city, Muhammad had religious visions and received from Allah the first verse of the Qur'an (Koran). He returned to Mecca in 630 and expelled all those who rejected the Islamic faith. To this day, the city is open only to Muslims.

The al Haram mosque was subsequently built. The Kaaba, in the center of the mosque's courtyard, is considered a replica of Allah's house in heaven. It holds the Black Stone, which is believed to have fallen from heaven. The Kaaba is the center of the circumambulations done by pilgrims, and it is toward the Kaaba that Muslims always face their prayers. This mosque, or house of worship, has space for approximately 300,000 worshippers. In the holy month of Ramadan, an additional 2 million Muslim pilgrims from around the world arrive in Mecca to worship, making it one of the most cosmopolitan cities on earth.

in order to gather military and political intelligence. Leblic traveled in disguise as an aristocratic Muslim, accompanied by many servants and with a variety of scientific instruments. His precise mission remains obscure, for he left little trace after reporting back to Paris in 1813. Leblic was followed to Mecca in 1809 by Ulrich Jasper Seetzen, who completed the hajj in the secret service of Czar Alexander I of Russia. Seetzen was a distinguished botanist and a scholar of Arabic who had already traveled in the region and was perhaps the best-prepared European explorer on the peninsula up to that time. Under orders from the czar, Seetzen was to continue his journey to Central Asia, but he was mysteriously murdered before he could leave Arabia. In 1814, Swiss Johann Ludwig Burckhardt reached Mecca on behalf of the British, in the course of a remarkably long route to the Niger River in Africa.

Burckhardt was born in Switzerland and educated in Germany. After completing his university education, he went to Britain with a letter of introduction to Sir Joseph Banks. This was the same Banks who had accompanied Captain Cook on his first voyage to the Pacific. He had subsequently become a leader of the scientific community in Britain, rising to the presidency of the British Royal Academy. In

The holiest city of the Islamic faith, Mecca is open only to Muslims. Many gather annually at the shrine of the Kaaba in the al Haram mosque's courtyard there, as they are in this 1880s photograph. *(Library of Congress, Prints and Photographs Division [LC-USZ62-99278])*

pursuing his wide-ranging interests, he had also founded the Association for Promoting the Discovery of the Interior Parts of Africa. He was impressed by the young Burckhardt and in due course arranged for the association to sponsor him on an exploratory mission. The ultimate objective of this mission was the discovery of the source of the Niger River in Africa. Burckhardt was not, however, to travel to the source of the river from its mouth on the west coast of Africa, but rather through the Middle East and North Africa.

In comparison with the elaborate preparations for other expeditions, Burckhardt's preparations appear quaint, if not naive. For six weeks prior to his departure, he attended an assortment of academic lectures on topics ranging from botany to astronomy, he studied Arabic, and he took long walks without a hat. He departed in 1809 for Syria, pausing for two months at Malta in order to improve his Arabic and assemble his disguise as an Indian Muslim trader. He then sailed on to Aleppo, where he stayed for longer than two years to become fluent in Arabic. He also traveled through Syria and Palestine and even located the ruins of the ancient city of Petra in present-day Jordan.

After further travels in Palestine and Egypt, Burckhardt sailed to Arabia in 1814 disguised as an Egyptian gentleman and pilgrim, using the name Ibrahim ibn Abdallah. Upon his arrival at Jeddah, he experienced serious financial difficulties, because the local bankers would not recognize his letters of credit from Egyptian bankers, largely because Burckhardt, in both disguise and in a bedraggled state of fatigue, did not look the part of a pilgrim worthy of credit. Fortunately, Burckhardt was befriended by Muhammad 'Ali, pasha of Egypt, who was then in Arabia waging a military campaign against the Wahhabi. Burckhardt informed Ali that he wanted to visit

Mecca as a Muslim pilgrim. The pasha was liberal in his religious views, so he offered his consent on the condition that Burckhardt demonstrate a Muslim's knowledge of Islamic theology. Burckhardt promptly passed an exam by two scholars of Islamic law and recited a long chapter from the Koran. He was therefore permitted to perform the rites of the hajj, which he did with respect and reverence for his extraordinary opportunity. He remained in Mecca for a total of four months, then visited the other major holy site of the Hijaz, the city of Medina, where the prophet Muhammad formed his first community and was later buried. Having spent several years in the Middle East, presumably on his way to Africa, Burckhardt finally turned to his preparations for an expedition to locate the source of the Niger River. Before he could begin, he contracted dysentery and died in Cairo in 1817. He was buried in a Muslim cemetery, his grave marked by the name of the pilgrim, Ibrahim ibn Abdallah.

Burckhardt's visits to the Muslim holy sites would be followed by other Europeans, the most famous of whom was Richard Burton. As a lieutenant in the Army of India, Burton had been drawn to Islam and developed a keen interest in visiting the Muslim holy sites. He gained support from the East India Company by proposing to travel to Arabia in search of horses for the army's cavalry. He then gained the support of the Royal Geographical Society by proposing to travel "for the purpose of removing that opprobrium [i.e., disgrace] to modern adventure, the huge white blob which in our maps still notes the Eastern and Central regions of Arabia." He studied Arabic for one year, then in 1853 traveled as an Afghani named Mirza Abdullah to Medina and Mecca. In contrast to Burckhardt, Burton recounted his travels in sensational prose, describing battles against thieves and his own personal

Sir Austen Henry Layard
(1817–1894)

The early European exploration of Arabia and the holy cities of Islam corresponded with important European explorations to the north, in the region of Mesopotamia, which is now known as Iraq. Sir Austen Henry Layard took a leading role in discovering and excavating the great biblical cities of Mesopotamia, though he had no formal training as an archaeologist. In fact, Layard worked as a lawyer in London before he quit his job in 1839 to join a friend in riding on horseback through Syria and other parts of what is now called the Middle East. Layard became intrigued by the ancient civilizations of the Mesopotamia and began his excavations at Nimrud, the site of the Assyrian capital of Calah, between 1845 and 1847. After discovering the remains of royal palaces at Nimrud, he shifted his work to a site near Mosul, in present-day Iraq, where he unearthed parts of the ancient biblical city of Nineveh, including the royal library of King Assurbanipal. It is noteworthy that archaeological research in Mesopotamia owed much to the same Carsten Niebuhr who transformed Europeans' perception of Arabia. On his way from India to Europe, Neibhur stopped in Persia in 1765 and collected ancient inscriptions, which later sparked European scholars' interest in the lost biblical cities and ancient civilizations of Mesopotamia.

Austen Henry Layard excavated, among other sites in Mesopotamia, the ancient biblical city of Nineveh, near Mosul, Iraq. *(Library of Congress, Prints and Photographs Division [LC-USZ62-128726])*

quest to understand "the inner life of the Muslim." He published his *Personal Narrative of a Pilgrimage to Al-Madinah and Meccah* to instant acclaim in 1855. The book became a best-seller, coming out in four editions during Burton's lifetime, and in many more since. Despite the dubious scientific merits of Burton's work, he did far more than any other European in the 19th century to promote popular interest in Arabia, particularly through his brilliant translation of *The Book of a Thousand Nights and a Night,* a series of Arabic folktales. His eye for the sensational and his unabashed self-promotion rendered Burton a controversial figure among other explorers of his day. Charles Doughty, for one, traveled simply and without fanfare among the Bedouin in the 1870s. Given his refusal to conceal his Christianity, he regularly suffered hardships ranging from robbery to imprisonment, but he survived to publish his masterfully crafted *Travels in Arabia Deserta.* Doughty regarded Burton as a publicity hound, and many later European explorers and devotees of Arabia came to agree with this view. T. E. Lawrence, better known as Lawrence of Arabia, regularly visited Doughty, whom he regarded as the doyen of Arabian explorers, until Doughty's death in 1926.

TRAVERSING THE PENINSULA

The first European to cross the Arabian Peninsula did so by accident, rather than by design. Captain George Sadlier of Her Majesty's 47th Foot regiment was sent from India in 1819 on a diplomatic mission to the Egyptian military commander Ibrahim Pasha. Sadlier was to congratulate the pasha on his suppression of a rebellion in Arabia and to propose joint action against the pirates of Muscat, who were then a threat to European shipping in the Sea of Oman. He sailed into the Persian Gulf and landed on the east coast of the peninsula, but unfortunately missed the pasha as the Egyptian forces moved west. After three months of chasing the pasha and his army, Sadlier caught up with them at Medina, from which he proceeded to Yanbu and then sailed back to India via the Red Sea. By all accounts, Sadlier would have gladly foregone the honor of crossing the Arabian Peninsula, for he detested the place and its peoples.

A far more enthusiastic William Gifford Palgrave became the first European to travel eastward across the peninsula in 1862. Palgrave had been educated at Oxford and commissioned as a lieutenant in the 8th Bombay regiment of the Army of India. During his service in India, he converted to Catholicism and was ordained a Jesuit priest in Madras. He resigned from the army to work as a missionary in India, then in 1853 he transferred his missionary work to Syria. He was forced to flee Syria after a massacre of Christians at Damascus in 1861, but he returned just a year later to undertake a journey through central Arabia. For this journey he disguised himself as a Syrian doctor, going by the name Mahmoud el-Eys. He was working not only for Pope Pius IX but also for the French ruler, Napoleon III (Louis-Napoleon). The former was interested in the prospects for spreading Christianity in the Middle East, and the latter wanted to know about prospects for alliances with Arab leaders and for trade in Arabian horses. Both the pope and Napoleon III were anticipating the completion of the Suez Canal in 1869, which would significantly improve European access to the Arabian Peninsula and to the region at large.

Palgrave and another Catholic priest departed from the west coast city of Ma'an on camels, accompanied by a guide and several servants. Palgrave's memoir, *A Year's Journey through Central and Eastern Arabia,* conveys the discomfort and frustration of traveling in a camel caravan. Palgrave was especially determined to dispel the Englishman's vision of a pleasurable excursion upon a "docile camel." "If 'docile' means stupid," Palgrave declared, "well and good; in such a case the camel is the very model of docility." According to Palgrave,

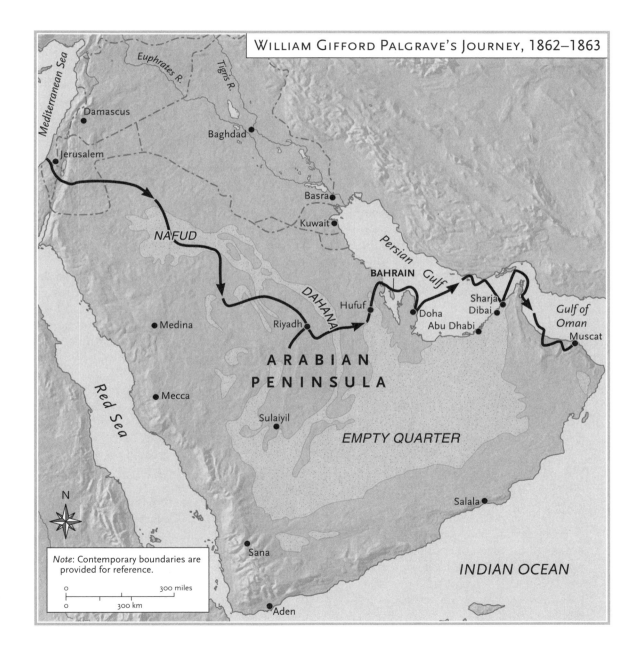

WILLIAM GIFFORD PALGRAVE'S JOURNEY, 1862–1863

"[The Camel] will never attempt to throw you off his back, such a trick being far beyond his limited comprehension; but if you fall off, he will never dream of stopping for you, and walks on just the same, grazing while he goes, without knowing or caring an atom what has become of you."

Palgrave and his party paused at the oases of Jauf, where they hired a guide to take them across the red sands of the Nafúd desert. At this time, central Arabia was divided between warring factions, as the Sa'udi dynasty attempted to maintain its dominance over the region. Palgrave stopped for three weeks in Ha'il to confer with Talal Ibn Rashid, a potential power broker. He then went on to Riyadh, the capital of the house of Sa'ud. Although the Sa'udis were prepared to deal with him, the religious leaders among the Wahhabi were deeply suspicious of Palgrave's intentions. He stayed in Riyadh for almost six weeks under increasingly threatening circumstances. As usual during his travels, he provided medical care to those in need, and his medical skills soon came to the attention of a member of the Sa'udi royal family, Prince 'Abd-Allah. The prince asked Palgrave to provide him with poison, which he probably intended to administer to his brother, his archrival. When Palgrave refused, the prince called him to his palace. Palgrave recounted the interview:

> After an interval of silence, 'Abd-Allah turned half round towards me, and with his blackest look and a deep voice said, "I now know perfectly well what you are; you are no doctors, you are Christians, spies, and revolutionists come hither to ruin our religion and state on behalf of those who sent you. The penalty for such as you is death, that you know, and I am determined to inflict it without delay.

With great poise, Palgrave denied the prince's charges and managed to bluff his way out of the palace. He and his companions remained in Riyadh for two more days, quietly assembling their belongings, then fled the city. They made it to the east coast and immediately boarded a ship to safety. In just a few years, Palgrave left the Jesuit order to become a British diplomat in northeast Africa and the Middle East. He died of bronchitis as the minister-resident in Uruguay in 1888, having returned once more to the Catholic faith.

ARISTOCRATS IN SEARCH OF HORSES

William Palgrave's dangerous encounters in Arabia stand in peculiar contrast to the experiences of an aristocratic couple, Sir Wilfrid and Lady Anne Blunt, who traveled easily through the deserts of the Arabian Peninsula, despite the intrigues and violence around them. Lady Anne had been born Anne King Noel, the granddaughter of Lord Byron, one of the great British poets of the 19th century. She had been raised in the most fashionable and intellectual circles of high society, becoming an accomplished artist and architect, as well as a well-respected writer. She married a fellow aristocrat, Wilfrid Blunt, in 1869, and Blunt soon inherited the estate at Crabbet Park, which provided the couple with comfortable wealth for the rest of their lives.

In the mid-1870s the Blunts traveled in Egypt, the Sinai, and Jerusalem. They would undertake their first serious expedition into the Middle East in 1878, when they assembled a large camel caravan at Aleppo and marched inland in search of horses. They departed from the coast of Syria on the Mediterranean and followed the Euphrates River eastward to

Baghdad. They then traveled north, picking up the Tigris River until Shergha, where they turned west. At the Khabur River they then veered southwest to Damascus, then back to the Mediterranean coast. In their return to the coast, Lady Anne became the first European woman to visit the Nejd on the Arabian Peninsula.

There were several bloody wars among the Bedouins in the regions of the Blunts' travels. The couple was more concerned, however, about the threat of a Bedouin raiding party, known as a ghazú. Although a ghazú customarily set out to steal camels and livestock from other tribes, the Blunts' caravan made an attractive, alternative prize. Lady Anne felt certain that they could fight off a ghazú of up to 15 men. After all, she reasoned, the Bedouin had only lances and old pistols, whereas Wilfrid carried a Winchester rifle that could fire 14 cartridges without being reloaded. If their caravan met a larger threat, the Blunts were prepared simply to abandon their possessions. As Lady Blunt coolly reflected in her travel memoir, *Bedouin Tribes of the Euphrates* (1879):

> At the worst, according to every account, there is no fear of being personally ill-treated; for the Arabs only care about plunder, and the utmost misfortune that could happen to us, if captured, would be to be stripped of some of our clothes, and left to find our way on foot to the nearest inhabited place—not a cheerful prospect, certainly, by still not altogether desperate.

The Blunts took a sympathetic view toward the Bedouin, attributing much of their violence to the Ottoman policy of exploiting internecine warfare among the tribes. Aside from her concerns about raiding parties, Lady Anne was impressed by Bedouin hospitality. The Bedouin did, in fact, observe strict rules of social etiquette. "They look upon hospitality not merely as a duty imposed by divine ordinance," she observed, "but as the primary instinct of the well-constituted mind. To refuse shelter or food to a stranger is held to be not merely a wicked action, an offence against divine or human law, but the very essence of depravity."

Lady Anne recognized that they faced far greater threats from the desert, which on more than one occasion appeared to be, as she put it, "a simmering furnace." The greatest dangers were to become lost or to run out of water between the wells that marked the caravan routes. In *Bedouin Tribes* Lady Anne recalled one incident when she and Wilfrid realized that their caravan was about to become separated:

> It was just about noon, and the mirage in the middle of the day quickly swallows up even a caravan of camels on the horizon, or they get hidden in a dip of the plain, and ours were now out of sight. Wilfrid and I galloped on to keep up the line of communication, which it is very dangerous to lose in traveling in the desert; and it was well we did so, for by the time we sighted them the rest of our straggling party was, in its turn, lost to view.

Lady Anne rode ahead to stop the caravan, and when Wilfrid rode back to collect the stragglers, he found that they had veered off in the wrong direction.

The Blunts did not rely upon tools of navigation in the desert. Instead, they employed the methods of the Bedouin. They would march toward a "tell," a distinctive feature on the horizon that could keep them on a relatively straight course. They also learned to

The Bedouin

The Bedouin are people of the various migratory tribes on the Arabian Peninsula, and in Negev and the Sinai. The word *Bedouin* is derived from an Arabic word, *Bedu,* which means simply "inhabitants of the desert" and does not imply a single ethnic, clan, or tribal group. The Bedouins share in common their migratory way of life and a mixed economy. They cultivate land during the growing period, and during the remainder of the year they herd camels, cattle, sheep, and goats.

In pre-Islamic Arabia, the Bedouin exercised considerable authority. Most significant was a Bedouin tribal kingdom, Kindah, which was located in the southern part of the Arabian Peninsula in present-day Yemen. Since the end of World War I, when many of the contemporary states, or at least the political boundaries, of the Middle East were established, the Bedouin have found themselves in conflict with modern political organizations. Bedouins are scattered among several states in the contemporary Middle East, including Egypt, Israel, Saudi Arabia, Iraq, Syria, and Jordan. The Bedouin are a small minority group in each country, often with little power. They nonetheless sustain their tribal organizations.

The Bedouin, such as the three men in this photograph, share a migratory way of life. *(Library of Congress, Prints and Photographs Division [LC-USZ62-76257])*

make use of the sun and the wind. "The shadow of one's horse's neck makes an excellent dial," Lady Anne explained, "and with a little practice it is easy to calculate the rate at which it ought to move round so that the course should be a straight one. The wind, too, in this country almost always blows northwest, and does not shift about in the plain, as it would among hills."

The Blunts were successful in their search for horses. They visited Deyr on the Euphrates, which was in Lady Anne's opinion "by far the best market for thorough breds in Asia." They returned to England with six Arabian mares, with which they began the Crabbet Arabian Stud farm in the same year. They subsequently returned to northern Arabia and the Nejd, and Lady Anne continued to write books and articles that provoked interest about Arabia in Europe. In 1882 the Blunts purchased a large home just outside Cairo, enabling both to spend more time in the Middle East and to acquire more horses for the Crabbet Stud. While based in Cairo, they acquired an additional 16 Arabian stallions and 51 mares. Crabbet would become a legendary stud farm in the world of Arabian horse breeding, and Lady Anne would write classic studies of Arabian horses along with her engaging travel narratives.

Lady Anne died in Cairo in December 1917, and Sir Wilfrid died on the Crabett estate in 1922. According to her obituary in the *Times* of London, at the age of 77, Lady Anne could still vault unassisted on to a horse.

WAR AND EXPLORATION

From the 18th century until the early 20th century, the European exploration of Arabia was largely influenced by the rise of the Wahhabi movement and the Sa'ud dynasty, the declining fortunes of the Ottoman Empire, and dynastic and tribal warfare. This political landscape changed dramatically between the outbreak of World War I in 1914 and the peace settlement signed between the Allies and the Ottoman Empire in 1920. The Ottomans joined the war on the side of Germany in October 1914, making enemies of Great Britain, the British Empire, and France. The British had not planned to fight the Ottomans, but they had no choice after October, given that they had become dependent on oil in the Ottoman territories in the Middle East. Most important, the British Royal Navy switched from coal to oil in fueling its ships after 1909, and it had begun to draw most of this oil from Persia. In response to the Ottoman declaration of war, the British captured virtually all the Ottoman territories in the Middle East by the end of 1917. The British also helped to organize a revolt by Arabs against the Ottomans after June 1916. The revolt was led by the ruler of the Hejaz, Sharif Husayn, who was a Hashimite with aspirations to rule all of Arabia. The Arab forces were assisted by T. E. Lawrence, who led Arab guerrillas in attacks on Turkish forces and installations. After the war, as before, Lawrence would return to Britain to consult with two of his idols, Charles Doughty and Sir Wilfrid Blunt.

The Sa'ud dynasty in central Arabia did not participate in the Arab rebellion, but effectively played the Ottomans and the British against each other to its own advantage. Harry St. John Bridger Philby was sent to Riyadh in 1917 to try to persuade Ibn Sa'ud to abandon his neutral position and attack the Rashidis, his old enemies, who were pro-Turkish. Although Philby failed to persuade Sa'ud to fight for the British, the two men struck up a friendship and conceived a plan to display Sa'ud's authority. Philby's superiors had indicated that he should not travel to the west coast due to the dangerous state of the country. The Sa'udi king arranged for a camel caravan and an armed escort to take Philby across the peninsula anyway, which Philby then did between December 9 and a few days after Christmas. Although this was a political stunt, it was also, from a geographical standpoint, the southernmost European crossing of the peninsula to date. In 1918, Philby undertook another expedition, surveying the peninsula all the way south to the northern edge of the Empty Quarter.

The British supported the power of the Hashemites in the Hejaz after the war, provoking strong criticism from Philby, who was thoroughly devoted to Ibn Sa'ud as Arabia's best hope for political stability. In protest against British policy, Philby resigned from the colonial service in 1925 and became a merchant in Jeddha. In the same year, Sharif Husayn was overthrown by Ibn Sa'ud, who had grown jealous of Husayn's favored status with the British. Two years later, the British recognized Sa'ud's sovereignty over the Hejaz. Sa'ud then set about crushing a civil war among Wahhabi factions who believed he was betraying their cause in working with the Christian British and in centralizing power in his own hands. The civil war concluded in 1930 when the British captured the rebel leaders in Kuwait and turned them over to Sa'ud for execution and other forms of punishment. He declared the kingdom of Saudi Arabia in 1932, unifying the Hejaz and the Najd for the first time in centuries. Over the next decade, Philby was instrumental in negotiating the opening of Saudi Arabia to oil exploration by U.S. companies. He assisted in founding the Arabian American Oil Company, which located massive oil reserves that would bring the Sa'udi dynasty spectacular wealth after World War II.

Philby was pleased to assist the king, but he did not aspire to be an oil executive. Instead, he wanted to achieve fame as an explorer, and he saw in Saudi Arabia's Empty Quarter the last blank space on the world's map requiring investigation. Since 1925, Philby had been attempting to get Sa'ud's approval for the first crossing of the Empty Quarter, but Sa'ud had been busy with civil wars and other burdens of a would-be head-of-state. In the meantime, in 1931, Bertram Thomas arrived at Doha to complete the first crossing of the Empty Quarter—a startling achievement that prompted Philby to lock himself in a room for a week in despair. Thomas had long experience in the Middle East, both as a British official and a minister to the sultan of Muscat and Oman. He had made preliminary journeys into the Empty Quarter, and he undertook his crossing with a serious view toward scientific studies of the desert's flora and fauna. After receiving virtually every major award in the field of exploration, he then published a travel memoir, *Arabia Felix,* about his journey. T. E. Lawrence observed in his introduction to the book: "Today we know the whole earth. Would-be wandering youth will go unsatisfied till a winged generation lands on the next planet."

As Thomas's expedition set off each morning in the Empty Quarter, the men declared, "In the name of God, the Compassionate, the Merciful." In addition to the mercy of Allah, Thomas's careful forethought, as well as some good fortune, made the expedition a success. Thomas anticipated that the heat and the terrain would take their toll on the camels and the men. The terrain of the Empty Quarter alternates between fine sand, gravel, and rock, providing very little water or pasture for many miles at a stretch. The "hungry marches" of nine to 10 hours were especially hard on the

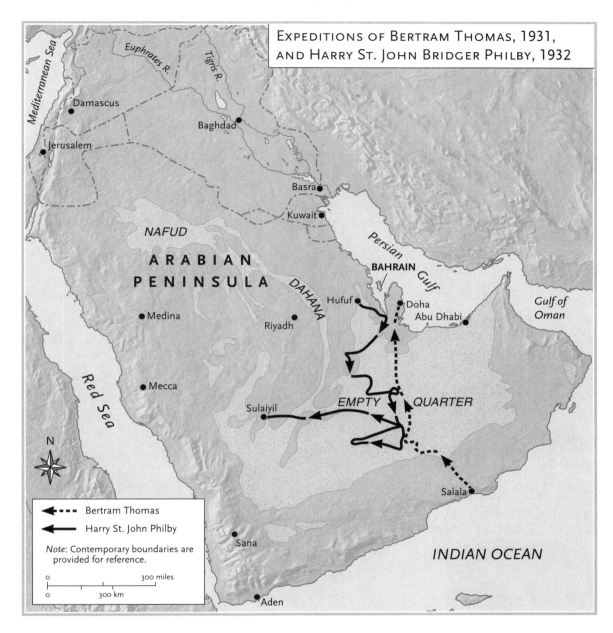

EXPEDITIONS OF BERTRAM THOMAS, 1931, AND HARRY ST. JOHN BRIDGER PHILBY, 1932

camels. Consequently, Thomas arranged for a fresh set of camels and men to await him at a point before the last difficult stretch of desert to the north.

Thomas's good fortune was to avoid ambush by the hostile Bedouin that traveled through the Empty Quarter. Regarding the Bedouin, Thomas observed:

They live mainly on camel's milk and hold life cheap. Raiding to them is the spice of life, and there was never a man in any of my escorts who had not raided into the Hadhramaut, nor one who had not been raided in his own grazing grounds, and some bore honorable scars of bullet or dagger wounds. Arms and ammunition and the health of the camel are thus the primary necessities of life; where hereditary blood-feuds divide the tribes, might is right, and man ever walks in fear for his life and possessions.

Travels in the Middle East sparked memoirs from various individuals. Freya Stark, seated at her desk, first traveled as an infant with her parents and chronicled her experiences in many places, including the Middle East, in books written throughout her life. *(National Archives of Canada)*

He was particularly fearful of the Sa'ar tribe, which was also a concern of Ibn Sa'ud in his deliberations over Philby's proposed crossing of the Empty Quarter. "The Sa'ar tribe and its allies are to-day the serious menace to peace in the southern sands," stated Thomas. "Numerically powerful—perhaps two thousand rifles—they derive strength from their remoteness, and have hitherto refused to receive an embassy from Bin Sa'ud."

For all the hardship endured across the Empty Quarter, Thomas reflected regularly upon the beauty of this inhospitable landscape. As they passed into a region of great red dunes, he was struck by the play of color in the midday light:

> No contrasting shades are afforded by the sun's almost vertical rays in this tropical latitude, and the resulting impressions are soft planes and an exquisite purity of colour. So smooth from a distance, the sands are in reality lined with faint coruscations like tiny wavelets on the shore, and what from afar is a sheet of pure red colour, when approached sparkles with glints of green and gold.

Philby may not have been the first European to cross the Empty Quarter, but he certainly proved to be the most thorough. On his first successful crossing, during which he carefully surveyed his route, he ignored Thomas's direct course and took perhaps the longest and most grueling route available. After proceeding south into the Empty Quarter to Nayfah, he then led his expedition west, more than 1,250 miles to Mecca. In the process of achieving fame as an explorer, Philby assisted Ibn Sa'ud in mapping his new

kingdom, a kingdom that would henceforth resist the influence of European empires. When the next significant European explorer, Wilfrid Thesiger, entered the Empty Quarter in the 1940s, it was not to define political boundaries, but to find the supposed breeding grounds of the locust. His travel memoir, *Arabian Sands,* was perhaps the first classic work of travel literature in the post-imperial era.

The European exploration of the Arabian Peninsula was initially driven by a combination of scientific curiosity, strategic imperial objectives, and a desire for adventure. By the 1930s, the primary motives were adventure and, especially in the case of Philby, an intense desire for fame. In the years between the two world wars, exploration on the peninsula was largely approved and directed not by European governments, but by Arab rulers who used the findings to serve their own political objectives. The next great era of exploration would not be geographical, but geological, and the Saudi royal family would turn from Europeans to Americans for assistance. The creation of the Arabian American Oil Company, facilitated by Philby in the service of the Saudis, set the stage for aggressive oil exploration on the peninsula. Whereas European geographical exploration had proceeded throughout decades of political instability in Arabia, oil exploration has proceeded under the firm political control of the Saudis, who have built fortunes upon oil since the 1950s. Remarkably, this new era of exploration on the Arabian Peninsula is not a legacy of European imperial exploration, but rather a product of Ibn Sa'ud's extraordinary ability to manipulate the British Empire and one of its most talented explorers to serve his own ends.

7

EXPLORING THE
TOP OF THE WORLD

The Himalayan peoples of Tibet and Nepal initially regarded the European mountaineers as crazy. They could not understand why Europeans would spend months organizing expeditions laden with heavy equipment, then suffer and risk death to climb the highest mountain peaks. The Himalayan peoples had no choice but to travel among the mountains every day. Their objective was not to ascend the highest peaks but to find the lowest and easiest passes through which to bring their herds of yaks to grazing grounds, to conduct their trade, and to maintain relations with neighboring villages. In the minds of the Himalayan peoples, the mountains did not have significance because they were tall but because they were the homes of the gods—and the highest peaks were not the homes of the greatest gods. Whereas Europeans became fascinated by the two highest Himalayan peaks, which they would name Mount Everest and K2, the Nepalis regarded the summit of the smaller Mount Kailas as far more important because it

was the home of the god Shiva. The Himalayan peoples never presumed to intrude upon the homes of the gods. Instead, they would walk around the bases of the sacred mountains to demonstrate their devotion and respect.

Mountaineering in the Himalayas involved climbers from many countries, but the British clearly took the lead until 1950. The British were initially drawn into the Himalayas not by a passion for mountaineering but by their imperial competition with Russia, known as the Great Game. Extending for approximately 1,500 miles across the northern border of India, the Himalayas were a crucial boundary between the British Empire in India and the steadily expanding Russian Empire to the north. In the interest of defending this boundary, the British dispatched numerous Indian surveyors, called pundits, to map the Himalayas after the 1860s, despite the objections of the governments of Nepal and Tibet. In the course of this massive survey project, the surveyor-general of India, Andrew Waugh, reported to the Royal Geographical Society in 1856 that Peak XV of the Himalayas was the highest mountain known to man, at 29,002 feet. This peak would subsequently become known as Mount Everest.

While the British, and Europeans in general, regarded the discovery of the highest mountain in the world as a valuable piece of geographical information, this information had no other obvious significance. The summit of Everest had no strategic value, and it certainly offered no hope for economic gain or colonial settlement. Moreover, at this time, the pressing interests of European geographers and explorers lay elsewhere, primarily in the rivers of Africa. In the same year that the Royal Geographical Society (RGS) learned that Peak XV was the highest in the world, it sent Richard Burton and John Hanning Speke to find the source of the Nile. If the RGS had an interest in mountains, it extended only to the rumored "Mountains of the Moon" in central Africa, from which the Nile supposedly flowed north into Egypt. In sum, the peaks of the Himalayas did not suit the priorities of European empires and explorations in the mid-19th century, because they had no value in terms of military objectives, commerce, Christianity, or even science. Mountaineering in this era remained a sport of wealthy Europeans who were content to test their limits in the Alps, the major European mountain range that rises in Austria, Switzerland, and Italy. By the turn of the century, however, the significance of the Himalayan peaks would begin to change and attract the interest of not only mountaineers but also British government officials.

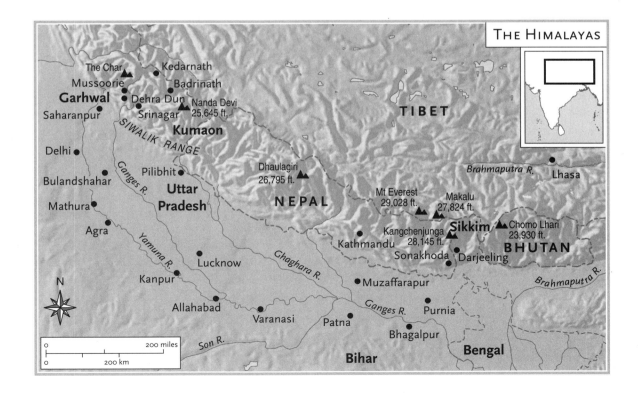

Sir George Everest

George Everest, an artillery officer in the Army of India, was assigned in 1818 to assist William Lambton in completing the Great Trigonometrical Survey of India. Lambton had begun the survey more than a decade earlier on the southern peninsula of the subcontinent. Upon Lambton's death, Everest took over as superintendent of the survey in 1823, and in 1830 he also became the surveyor-general of India. He oversaw the progress of the survey to the Himalayas at Dehra Dun, then conducted a longitudinal survey along the Nepalese border. This was meticulous, difficult, and generally miserable work, complicated by the constant threat of malaria, which claimed the lives of numerous employees of the survey. Everest's greatest achievement was the surveying of the Great Meridianal Arc of India, a task that occupied him from 1818 until his final computations in 1843, after which he retired. Five years later the Royal Astronomical Society awarded Everest high honors for his labors in India. Speaking at the ceremony, Sir John Herschel declared, "The Great Meridianal Arc of India is a trophy of which any nation, or any government of the world, would have reason to be proud, and will be one of the most enduring monuments of their power and enlightened regard for the progress of human knowledge."

In 1856 the next surveyor-general, Andrew Waugh, determined that Peak XV of the Himalayas was the highest mountain known to humans. In recognition of Everest's achievements in surveying India, it was proposed that Peak XV should be given his name. Everest himself advised against this, on the grounds that his name could literally not be pronounced by the people of India. Moreover, it was customary among geographers to recognize the local names of mountains in naming them for the official geographical record. British officials and a number of European explorers argued that different local names already existed for the mountain. There was, for instance, a great deal of evidence that the Tibetans called the mountain Chomolungma. It appears that Waugh and his supporters simply chose to ignore this evidence in the interest of honoring Everest. In 1865, upon Waugh's recommendation, the government of India decided to call the mountain "Everest." Sir Francis Younghusband reflected upon the name as he anticipated the first British expedition to the mountain in 1921. In the *Morning Post* in November 1920, Younghusband stated: "It would be a great misfortune if the beautiful and suitable name of Mt Everest was ever changed, even though it is . . . not a native name." He added, "Even if this proposed expedition finds its real name written clearly upon the mountain, I hope it will take no notice, as I am sure you will agree that no name is so beautiful and suitable as Mt Everest."

One can discern a new perspective upon the peaks of the Himalayas that developed between 1887 and 1921. In 1887, Lieutenant Francis Younghusband made his remarkable journey from Peking in China to India. As he approached India, he became the first European to travel through the Mustagh Pass. In his book, *Everest: The Challenge,* he recalls,

> As I was ascending the valley which led up to the Mustagh Pass . . . there suddenly came into view a sight which brought me to an immediate standstill, and made me gasp with amazement. It was a mountain unbelievably higher than anything I had imagined, and I was only a few miles from its base, so that I could realize its height to the full.
>
> I knew not what mountain it was; but I found afterwards that it was no other than K2, the second highest mountain in the world, 28,250 feet in altitude, and only 750 feet lower than Everest itself.

Two years later he returned to explore the region around K2, which featured additional high peaks that ranged from 25,000 to 27,000 feet in height. Younghusband observes, "My dominant feeling was one of delight—of joy at having had the chance of seeing so wonderful a sight." He added, ". . . Full of spirit as I was, the idea that I, or any one else, should presume to think of climbing any one of them never entered my mind." Younghusband subsequently became the president of the Royal Geographical Society and used his influence to assist in organizing the first Everest Reconnaissance Expedition in 1921.

In order to explain this shift in the British perspective upon the high peaks of the Himalayas, one must take into account two factors: the empire and airplanes. Over the course of the 19th century, Europeans had learned to regard triumphs in exploration as both instruments of imperial expansion and symbols of national greatness. By the start of the 20th century, with much of the world's exploration behind them, Europeans looked for new geographical objectives that might

not advance commerce, Christianity, or perhaps even science, but which would nonetheless symbolize their own superiority as a nation. It was this change in the priorities of exploration that enabled George Mallory to explain in 1923 that he desired to climb Everest "because it is there"—an answer that would have been incomprehensible to explorers of the 19th century. The British were conscious of the symbolic value of exploration, and especially so after they won the Great Game in Asia. In 1904, Colonel Francis Younghusband imposed the Anglo-Tibetan Convention upon the Tibetan government and thus preempted their alliance with the Russians. Soon thereafter, the Russians suffered a

The first European to travel through the Mustagh Pass, a route between China and India, Francis Younghusband later became president of the Royal Geographical Society. *(Library of Congress, Prints and Photographs Division [LC-G412-T-9080-003])*

humiliating defeat by the Japanese navy in the Russo-Japanese War, which undermined Russia's authority in Asia as a whole. The viceroy of India, Lord Curzon, recognized that Britain had finally gained the upper hand in the Great Game, and he looked to the Himalayan peaks as potential symbols of Britain's dominance in the region. In 1905 he wrote to an influential member of the Alpine Club: "It has always seemed to me a reproach that with the second highest mountain in the world for the most part in British territory and with the highest in a neighboring and friendly state [i.e., Nepal], we, the mountaineers and pioneers par excellence of the universe, make no sustained and scientific attempt to climb to the top of either of them." Curzon proposed that the British government cooperate with the Alpine Club to organize an expedition to climb either Everest or K2, or, preferably, both. Although this proposal did not come to fruition, it marked a new attitude among British imperial officials toward mountaineering in the Himalayas.

Plans for climbing the highest Himalayan peaks only took shape after the armistice of World War I in 1918. The British saw the ascent of Everest, in particular, as an act that would reflect the greatness of the British nation, a greatness that was already mapped upon the postwar world. The British Empire reached its maximum size at the same time that the British launched their first expeditions to climb Everest in the 1920s. How could a mountain defy the will and skill of an empire upon which the sun never set?

It was not only imperial pride and ambition that contributed to the desire to climb Everest. After World War I, Europeans believed, as never before, that the ascent might be physically possible. The scholarly study of human physiology at high altitudes was a new science in the late 19th century. This science was significantly advanced by the advent of military aircraft during the world war of 1914–18. Although the European militaries were quick to see the value of aircraft in reconnaissance and, to a lesser extent, in bombing, they had no idea how high altitudes would affect the human body. When Europe's generals found that scientists shared their ignorance, they put money into scientific research. After the war, the findings of this research were turned from military uses to mountaineering. Still, no one had any idea how the human body would function for prolonged periods at extreme altitudes above 27,000 feet, or whether it would function at all at 29,000 feet, on the summit of Everest. Even as Edmund Hillary and Tenzing Norgay set off on their final assault on Everest's summit in 1953, assisted by oxygen tanks, they were not sure that their bodies would hold up on the top of the world. This issue was only resolved when Hillary removed his oxygen mask to take a photograph of Norgay on the summit.

EARLY MOUNTAINEERING IN THE HIMALAYAS AND THE KARAKORUM

Martin Conway was the first to combine scientific exploration and mountaineering in the Himalayas. He undertook an expedition to the Karakorum Mountains in Kashmir in 1892, hoping to climb K2 or another mountain of at least 25,000 feet. This was an ambitious plan because, at that time, it was commonly believed that humans could not survive at over 22,000 feet. Like Younghusband before him, and like many would-be climbers afterward, Conway reached K2 only to decide that the ascent of its seemingly sheer walls of rock and ice was impossible. Instead, he climbed 22,600 feet to the summit of Pioneer Peak, establishing a new altitude record. He also occupied himself by collecting plants and small animals and by producing a map of Karakorum, later published by the Royal Geographical Society. Younghusband had corresponded with Conway before his climbs and had been skeptical of his chances for success. Younghusband declared in retrospect that although Conway never reached 25,000 feet, ". . . he did set the mind of man towards attaining the supreme heights; and man has fastened on them ever since."

One of the men who accompanied Conway, a lieutenant in the Indian army named Charles Granville Bruce, would return to the Himalayan peaks as one of the leading British mountaineers of later years. Just one year after his expedition with Conway, Bruce met Younghusband at the British base at Chitral, and the two men climbed a local mountain, Ispero Zorn. It was during this meeting that Bruce proposed to Younghusband that they should consider an ascent of Mount Everest. This was the first proposal to climb Everest, but the two men pursued the idea no further.

In the ensuing years, an increasing number of European mountaineers arrived in the Himalayas, with a predictable mixture of success and failure. A well-known climber named Albert Mummery attempted to climb Nanga Parbat in Kashmir in 1895. At 26,620 feet, the mountain offered Mummery the chance to shatter all existing altitude records, but he never returned from the mountain, and his body was never found. In 1907 the team of Charles Bruce, Arnold Mumm, and Tom Longstaff traveled to Garhwal and climbed Trisul at 23,360 feet, decisively passing the 22,000-foot boundary. In 1909, an Italian, the duke of the Abruzzi, arrived in Kashmir with a large expedition to climb K2. When the expedition reached the mountain, they were awed not only by its size but also by its lack of any accessible route to the summit. After studying the mountain for some time, the duke attempted the climb with three Italian guides, four Italian porters, and some Indian porters as well. At 20,000 feet they were forced to turn back, but their failure on K2 produced two pieces of important information for the science of climbing at these unprecedented heights. First, they realized they could not possibly reach the summit of K2 in a single day, as was possible on the mountains of the Alps. Instead, climbers would have to establish a series of camps where they could spend a succession of nights before proceeding. This strategy would prove essential to the successful ascent of the highest peaks, and especially Mount Everest. Second, having retreated from K2, the duke succeeded in climbing 24,600 feet toward Bride Peak. Although he and his party did not reach the peak itself at 25,110 feet, they set a new altitude record and thus extended the boundaries of human endurance. A physician who accompanied the expedition declared afterward that altitude was not, after all, an obstacle to the ascent of the world's tallest mountains. This prediction would appear all the more reasonable with the advent of oxygen technology for mountaineers in the 1920s. The first ascent of Everest without the assistance of oxygen technology would not take place until 1978.

The most important European mountaineer in the Himalayas before World War I did not set an altitude record. Dr. Alexander Mitchell Kellas was a lecturer in chemistry at Middlesex Hospital who first traveled to the Himalayas in 1907. Over the next several years, he would climb mountains in Tibet, Kashmir, and Sikkim, including Mount Pauhunri at 23,180 feet. Kellas did not travel with Europeans, but only with Tibetans and Sherpas, the latter being from the area of the Khumbu Valley in Nepal. Kellas was one of the first scientists to study the affects of high altitudes on human physiology, and he was struck by the remarkable strength of his porters. He conducted studies of the Tibetans and Sherpas during their climbs, testing their breathing and their heart rates at high altitudes. He came to the conclusion that the physiology of these people had become acclimated to high altitudes to a greater extent than Europeans could hope to become, and he proposed that they would make ideal porters for mountaineers at the highest altitudes.

Up to this point, Europeans had generally relied upon other Europeans, Indians, Gurkhas, and Hindu Nepalis to act as their porters. Preference was commonly given to the Nepalis, who traveled to Darjeeling in India to work as porters and manual laborers in construction projects and on tea plantations. Kellas began to train Tibetans and Sherpas in advanced climbing techniques, and they quickly proved themselves to be not only superior porters but also skilled climbers. Kellas brought four Sherpas with him on the British Reconnaissance Expedition to Everest in 1921. He died of a combination of dysentery and heart failure before reaching the base of the mountain, but his advocacy of Himalayan porters was nonetheless supported by the fine performances of his porters. After the 1920s, sherpas would become the elite high-altitude porters of the Himalayas.

In the years before the outbreak of World War I in 1914, the British came to regard Mount Everest as the great prize of moun-

---

Sherpas 〜

In the 15th or 16th centuries, people from southeastern Tibet migrated to the eastern Himalayas, in what is now Nepal. These people became known as the Sherpa, meaning "the people from the east." The Sherpas were originally composed of 18 separate clans, which eventually dispersed beyond Nepal to Darjeeling in India and Bhutan. Sherpas have long played a vital role in exploration and mountaineering in the Himalayas, due to their strength and endurance at high altitudes. It is noteworthy that in the early 20th century, Europeans began to use the word *sherpa* as a general description of any porter who accompanied them on a climb, so it is sometimes difficult to determine from historical records the ethnicity of particular porters.

Historically, the Sherpas grazed yak herds and grew potatoes and barley, and they saw the mountains as sacred places where the gods resided. They turned to working as porters for European mountaineers because they found they could make far more money as porters than as herders and farmers. Even as Sherpas began to ascend the highest mountain peaks in the 1920s, Buddhist lamas commonly urged them not to set foot on summits, as this would offend the gods. In 1938 the Himalayan Club began to award the Tiger Medal to Sherpas who climbed to the highest altitudes. According to Tenzing Tashi, the grandson of Tenzing Norgay and a climber of Everest himself, this remains for Sherpas the ultimate mountaineering prize.

taineering, but political issues stood in their way. The government of Nepal was openly hostile to European incursions, and the Tibetans were also opposed to European advances. In response to the threat of a Tibetan alliance with the Russians, a British military expedition marched to Lhasa in 1904 and imposed the Anglo-Tibetan Convention, which gave the British privileged but limited access to Tibet in the future. The leader of this British expedition, Colonel Younghusband, dispatched Captain C. G. Rawling and Captain C. H. D. Ryder on a reconnaissance mission to western Tibet. The British officers saw Everest from 60 miles away, and Rawling observed that it might be climbed by the North Ridge.

With Everest in sight, the Alpine Club and the Royal Geographical Society proposed a major expedition to climb the mountain in 1907. They even secured the full support of the viceroy of India, Lord Minto. However, John Morley, the secretary of state for India, blocked the expedition because he did not want to risk aggravating British relations with Tibet. It was therefore by default that Bruce, Mumm, and Longstaff traveled to Garhwal and climbed Trisul. Six years later, in 1913, a young British officer, John Noel, succeeded in traveling in disguise to within 40 miles of Everest—the closest that a European had been to the mountain to date. In August of the following year, Britain went to war against Germany, and all plans for mountaineering were postponed.

THE POSTWAR EXPEDITIONS TO EVEREST

After the armistice of 1918, the Alpine Club and the Royal Geographical Society (RGS) agreed to cooperate in making a successful ascent of Everest. Younghusband became the president of the RGS after the war, and he

formed the Mount Everest Committee, reconstituted as the Himalayan Committee in 1947, to support expeditions to the mountain. Although Nepal would still not authorize an expedition to Everest from the south, the British enjoyed a more favorable reception from the Tibetans. The Chinese had reasserted their control over Tibet in 1910, at which time the Dalai Lama, Thubten Gyatso, found sanctuary in India. Due to political unrest at home, the Chinese forces withdrew from Tibet in 1913, enabling the Dalai Lama to return with a more favorable view toward the British who had supported him in exile. Tibet would remain independent of Chinese control until 1950, providing a window of opportunity for British and other European climbers to make attempts on Everest and the other major Himalayan peaks.

In the 1920s, Darjeeling developed as a base from which Europeans assembled and staged their expeditions. Over the course of the decade, Sherpas traveled the 100 miles from the Khumbu region of Nepal to Darjeeling in increasing numbers, as it became clear that they could make far more money as porters than in herding yaks or growing potatoes and barley. By the mid-1920s there were thousands of Sherpas in residence at Darjeeling, doing odd jobs in the hope of joining a major expedition. In the first decade after the war, the recruitment process was haphazard at best, but the process was then systematized under the Himalayan Club, founded by the British in February 1928. Porters of all kinds (including Sherpas, Bhutias, and Tibetans) now received standard wages on a regulated scale, and their service was chronicled in books they were all required to carry. At the end of each expedition, each porter's book was signed by the expedition leader and the Himalayan Club secretary. In this way, porters were able to maintain a record of their

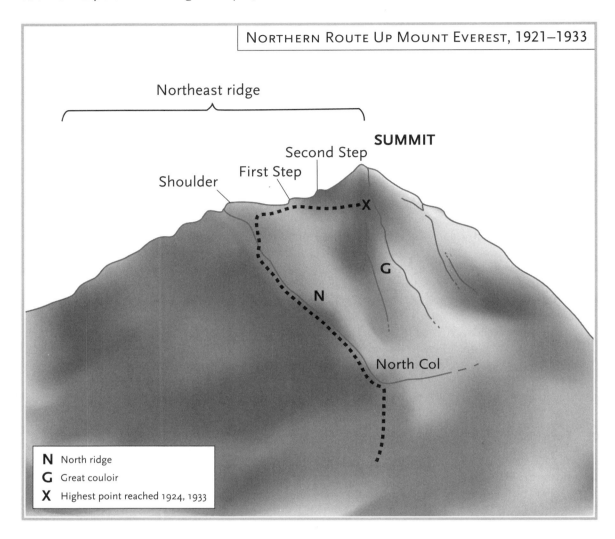

NORTHERN ROUTE UP MOUNT EVEREST, 1921–1933

Northeast ridge

SUMMIT

Second Step

First Step

Shoulder

X

G

N

North Col

N North ridge
G Great couloir
X Highest point reached 1924, 1933

achievements and receive higher wages in accordance with their experience.

The British launched their First Reconnaissance Expedition to Everest in 1921. Under the leadership of Charles Howard-Bury, this expedition was simply to evaluate possible paths of ascent up the mountain. These were the first Europeans to reach Mount Everest, and they were awed by its size and the potential difficulties of the climb. The

strongest climber on the expedition was George Leigh Mallory, a graduate of Cambridge University, a veteran of World War I, and a schoolmaster. At 35, Mallory already had a good deal of experience in climbing mountains in the Alps and the Himalayas, and he was in the best physical condition of his life. Having approached the mountain from the north, Howard-Bury sent Mallory up the Rongbuk Glacier to the mountain's north face.

From the glacier, Mallory saw a ridge that proceeded directly to the summit, but a series of sheer cliffs rendered his approach to the ridge impossible. He saw a gap in the cliffs, which would become known as the North Col, and he suspected that he might be able to reach the gap from another angle. Consequently, the expedition traveled around the mountain to attempt to reach the Col from the east. As Mallory had hoped, he was then able to climb an ice fall of about 1,200 feet to the Col, from which he looked up the north face to the summit. Although he was encouraged by the discovery of a seemingly direct path to the summit, he was also worried by the sight of ferocious winds to which the ridge was exposed. Despite the threat of the elements, this would be the approach taken by the first two British expeditions to attempt to climb Everest.

In 1922 the British sent their second expedition to Everest, this time to reach the summit by ascending the north ridge. The expedition was under the leadership of Charles Bruce, the same man who had first proposed climbing Everest in 1893. This expedition was the first to bring oxygen technology, which was overseen by George Finch. Following the early work of Kellas, this expedition included 40 Sherpas, in addition to local porters, and 300 pack animals. The expedition did not succeed in reaching the summit, but it nonetheless made significant gains. An assault team with oxygen technology reached 27,300 feet, a new altitude record, and another assault team without oxygen technology reached 26,800 feet.

This expedition provided European mountaineers with an opportunity to experience the full range of obstacles on Everest. The most obvious obstacle was the terrain of Everest itself, steep and often unstable, threatening an avalanche from above one's head or below one's feet. The terrain is then swept by sudden storms, which can rise from a blue sky and proceed quickly to hurricane conditions. Many climbers would compare the wind on Everest to the lashes of a whip. The wind can knock a climber off his or her feet, and it carries ice crystals that ice over a climber's goggles, leaving no option but to remove them. Without goggles, the climber's eyelashes then freeze together. Commonly, the wind brings blinding snow, which can force climbers to advance on their hands and knees. Of course, the wind only decreases the subzero temperatures, which regularly threaten to produce frostbite. Climbers often spoke of the peculiar feeling of numbness taking over their bodies, or their difficulty in breathing due to the cold. The cold created particular problems with food, because insulated thermoses could not keep liquids from freezing. The cold also made it difficult to boil water on the climbers' primus stoves, which were also frequently used to thaw frozen boots in the mornings. Finally, the lack of oxygen at altitudes over 24,000 feet created many problems, ranging from depression, to poor concentration, to impaired coordination.

The 1922 expedition was a valuable learning experience. The climbers especially learned to appreciate the potential value of oxygen technology in increasing their speed and endurance. Also, they learned that their bodies could, to a surprising extent, acclimate to higher altitudes, given enough time. Previously, scientists had speculated that the body would become weaker as it remained at a high altitude, but in fact the reverse appeared to be true. On the other hand, the climbers did not yet appreciate that there were diminishing returns on acclimatizing, given other factors, such as weather, fatigue, and disease, that took their toll on the body. The expedition also learned that they would

Altitude Sickness and Oxygen Technology ⁓

As one rises in altitude, one takes in a decreasing number of oxygen molecules with each breath. One experiences altitude sickness due to inadequate oxygen in one's body, a condition that can be avoided or at least improved by taking time to adapt to specific altitudes before preceding higher. There are different forms and degrees of altitude sickness. In its mild forms, altitude sickness results in dizziness, fatigue, and nausea. In its more severe forms, altitude sickness can result in fluid leaking from the capillaries—due to changes in pressure—and building up in the lungs or brain, producing symptoms including disorientation, hallucinations, and even death. Altitude sickness is a serious threat to climbers at extremely high altitudes, over 18,000 feet. In the early 20th century, doctors understood little about human physiology at high altitudes, but they began to consider this matter more closely with the deployment of airplanes in World War I. Alexander Kellas had intended to conduct experiments with oxygen during the 1921 expedition to Everest, but he died before the tests could be run. Members of the 1922 expedition then consulted with Professor G. Dreyer of Oxford University, who had studied this issue in the service of the Royal Air Force. He speculated that it would be necessary to use oxygen to reach and return from Everest's summit. The expedition brought different kinds of oxygen devices with them, and found that oxygen gas stored under pressure in steel cylinders was most effective. Unfortunately, a complete pack of four cylinders was relatively heavy, weighing 32 pounds. Furthermore, the climbers

have to pitch their final camp much closer to the summit. George Mallory had naively planned to locate the last camp at about 25,000 feet, leaving an impossibly long 4,000-foot dash to the summit on a single day. Apart from Mallory's particular misjudgment, it had not occurred to him, or other leading figures on the expedition, that Sherpas could carry supplies over 25,000 feet. In later attempts on Everest, a high priority would be placed upon establishing and supplying a final camp at a much higher altitude. The exertions and lessons of these expeditions could do nothing, however, to avert its great tragedy. An avalanche carried nine Sherpas over an ice cliff and into a deep crevasse. Although two miraculously survived long enough to be dug

out of the snow, seven died. The remaining Sherpas chose to leave the dead buried in the crevasse, in honor of their bravery on the mountain.

A second British expedition under the leadership of Charles Bruce attempted to reach the summit of Everest in 1924. In light of their experience two years before, the British ascended the north ridge and pushed the limits of the Sherpas' endurance to place their last camp, Camp VI, closer to the summit at 26,800 feet. A camp at this altitude provided a realistic, if not probable, chance of reaching the summit if the weather cooperated. There were two assault teams: Howard Somervell and Edward (E. F.) Norton, who would go first, and George Mallory and Sandy Irvine, found the oxygen masks to be inefficient and difficult to use because ice collected in the apparatus. Nonetheless, tests at high altitudes demonstrated that oxygen apparatus increased endurance, though the additional weight of the pack of cylinders compromised the benefits to an extent.

In the ensuing years, climbers attempted to decrease the weight of the oxygen packs and improve the masks. Most important, climbers experimented with open-circuit and closed-circuit breathing systems. In contrast to the standard open circuit, the closed circuit retrieved the oxygen not actually used by the climber, returning it to his or her supply. This meant that less oxygen was required, which decreased the weight of the pack. Proponents of the closed-circuit system also argued that it provided oxygen richer in quality. The proponents of the open-circuit system asserted that it had the supreme benefit of being easier to use and more reliable under the adverse conditions of extremely high altitudes. The two systems were compared on Everest for the first time during the 1938 expedition, but this did not end the debate. Nonetheless, the general credibility of oxygen-assisted climbing was established between the wars, and every member of the 1953 expedition expected to use oxygen. After much discussion, the 1953 expedition compromised by taking 12 open sets and eight closed sets for the ascent. Edmund Hillary and Tenzing Norgay were using open-circuit systems when they reached the summit on May 29, 1953. John Hunt, leader of the expedition, observed in his memoir, *The Ascent of Everest,* "But for oxygen . . . we should certainly not have got to the top."

whose fateful ascent would add both a mystery and a legend to the history of the mountain.

On June 5, Somervell and Norton made their bid for the summit, but they found their approach along the north ridge blocked by a sheer rock face. They attempted to go around the obstacle, working their way along the side of the mountain, balancing upon snow-covered slabs of rock that slanted like the tiles of a roof. It was a precarious and dangerous path, for if one fell there was nothing to break one's fall to a glacier 10,000 feet below. Although Somervell's fatigue forced him to give up, Norton proceeded alone to 28,126 feet, still short of the base of the final pyramid that caps the mountain. Fatigue and the late hour

of the day finally induced Norton to turn back, recognizing that he would otherwise die on the mountain. He met with Somervell, who waited on the ridge beyond the icy slabs of rock, and the two men then staggered down the mountain to join their colleagues at Camp IV. Due to his physical excursions at extreme altitude, Norton experienced intense pain in his eyes and went blind for 60 hours. He was still blind when he shook the hands of Mallory and Irvine as they proceeded up the north ridge to make the expedition's second assault on the summit.

Mallory and Irvine were an odd pair to be ascending the tallest mountain in the world. Whereas Mallory was an accomplished climber, and arguably the most fit man on the expedition, Irvine was a much younger man who had little previous experience in mountaineering. Regardless of the wisdom of this pairing, the men began their assault on the summit on June 8, as their colleagues below waited with apprehension. One of these colleagues, Noel Odell, could not resign himself to sitting nervously in Camp V, so he set off by himself to climb to Camp VI, pausing to conduct geological research at just over 26,000 feet on the North Face. As he climbed up through a crag, he saw the clouds clear on the summit and two figures moving along the ridge beneath the final summit pyramid. As Odell recalls in E. F. Norton's book, *The Fight for Everest: 1924:*

> I noticed far away on a snow slope leading up to what seemed to me to be the last step but one from the base of the final pyramid, a tiny object moving and approaching the rock step. A second object followed, and then the first climbed to the top of the step. As I stood intently watching this dramatic appearance, the scene became enveloped in cloud once more. . . .

Odell continued his climb to Camp VI, which he reached as a severe storm suddenly broke upon the mountain. He waited to assist Mallory and Irvine, but they did not return. He had another clear view of the summit later in the afternoon, but this time he saw no objects moving along the ridge. He descended to Camp V, then returned to Camp VI two days later, finding everything just as he had left it. Upon returning to Camp V, he made a pre-arranged signal to his colleagues below at Camp III, who could see Camp V through a telescope. He placed six blankets in the form of a cross, signaling "Death." The remaining members of the expedition were unable to locate and recover the bodies of Mallory and

Irvine, who were mourned in Britain as national heroes.

Ever since the disappearance of Mallory and Irvine, mountaineers and historians have debated whether, in fact, the two men reached the summit of Everest. It is improbable, given their primitive equipment, the sudden storm witnessed by Odell, and, of course, the mountain itself. There was, nevertheless, an intense, perhaps even romantic desire to hold out hope for some future proof of their success. When Edmund Hillary and Tenzing Norgay reached the summit of Everest in 1953, Hillary looked for any sign left by Mallory and Irvine but found nothing. Mallory's body was finally found in 1999, frozen face down to a slope beneath the precarious rock tiles, but his remains conveyed little about his success or failure in his attempt to reach the summit. He had broken his leg in a fall, and there was still a rope tied around his waist, suggesting that he and Irvine had been joined in their fate. Irvine's body has yet to be found, among many other fallen climbers still missing on the mountain. Despite the tragedy of Mallory and Irvine's death, however, it must be said that British climbers again gained valuable information during the 1924 expedition. They saw further evidence of acclimatization, as demonstrated by Noel Odell, who twice climbed to 27,000 feet and was 10 days above 23,000. They also saw that Sherpas could carry to an altitude regarded as unthinkable just a few years before.

The Tibetan government refused to authorize another British expedition to Everest until 1932. Under the leadership of Hugh Ruttledge, this expedition set off from Darjeeling in March 1933, well ahead of the standard departure date. It was Ruttledge's intention not to rely upon oxygen for the assault on the summit but to rely instead on slow acclimatization. Everest is best climbed between early

May and early June, in the month before the monsoon season begins. Ruttledge believed that a longer approach to the mountain would enable his climbers to gather, rather than lose, their strength. Unfortunately, the monsoons arrived two weeks early, bringing terrible weather to Everest before the expedition could properly prepare for the assault. The British and their Sherpa porters succeeded in establishing Camp VI at 27,400 feet, a full 600 feet higher than the last camp of the 1924 Expedition. On May 30, during a break in the weather, Wyn Harris and Lawrence Wager made their final assault on the summit, reaching within just 900 feet of the peak before they were stopped and turned back by impassible snow.

At the same time that the British were taking advantage of their privileged access to Everest, other European expeditions were attempting to climb the other highest peaks of the Himalayas. Two German expeditions, led by Dr. Paul Bauer, attempted and failed to climb Kangchenjunga, the third-highest mountain in the world, within sight of Darjeeling, in 1929 and 1931. There was also a disastrous 1934 German expedition, led by Willy Merkl, to climb Nanga Parbat in Kashmir. Due to terrible weather, four Germans and six porters died in their attempts to escape the mountain over the course of three days. Ang Tshering, a Sherpa, was the only survivor of the assault team. He made a last heroic climb down the mountain in an attempt to secure help for Merkl and another Sherpa, Gaylay, who had taken shelter in an ice cave due to Merkl's physical collapse. Tshering's efforts were in vain, and all his toes had to be amputated due to frostbite. He was awarded the Medal of Honor of the German Red Cross, the first time that a Sherpa received a foreign honor. There were, of course, small triumphs in the midst of the hardships of mountaineering between the wars. In 1930 a small British team under Frank Smythe climbed Kamet, 25,645 feet, the first summit over 25,000 feet. Not one of the highest peaks in the Himalayas had been conquered, however, before the outbreak of World War II in 1939.

THE FIRST ASCENT

British mountaineers were eager to return to Everest after the end of World War II in 1945. They soon recognized, however, that their plans would be delayed by India's rapid progress toward independence in August 1947, followed by the violent partition of the subcontinent between India and the new nation of Pakistan. At the same time, the Dalai Lama's horoscope was read, and it was determined that he would be threatened by foreigners in the near future. In response to this threat, Tibet once more closed its borders to foreigners, blocking any British expedition to Everest. In October 1950 the horoscope was proved accurate, when Communist China invaded and took over Tibet. This international crisis then produced an unexpected benefit for British mountaineers. Fears of Chinese expansion induced Nepal to open relations with the West and, more important, to open its borders to Europeans for the first time. Since 1921, the British had been approaching Everest from the north through Tibet. Now they saw the possibility of approaching the mountain through Nepal to the south.

The approach to Everest through Tibet had required expeditions to trek through barren lands and to make rapid ascents of high mountain passes. By contrast, the approach through Nepal took expeditions through fertile lands and beautiful forests, rising gradually and thus assisting the mountaineers in acclimatizing. Moreover, the approach through Nepal brought expeditions through the Khumbu valley, at the head of which stood the mountain. The Khumbu region was the home of the Sherpas.

An Anglo-American Reconnaissance Expedition was the first to explore the approach to Everest through the Khumbu valley in 1950. One year later the British undertook their own reconnaissance expedition, under the leadership of Eric Shipton. The primary purpose of the expedition was to determine if they could actually ascend the mountain from the south,

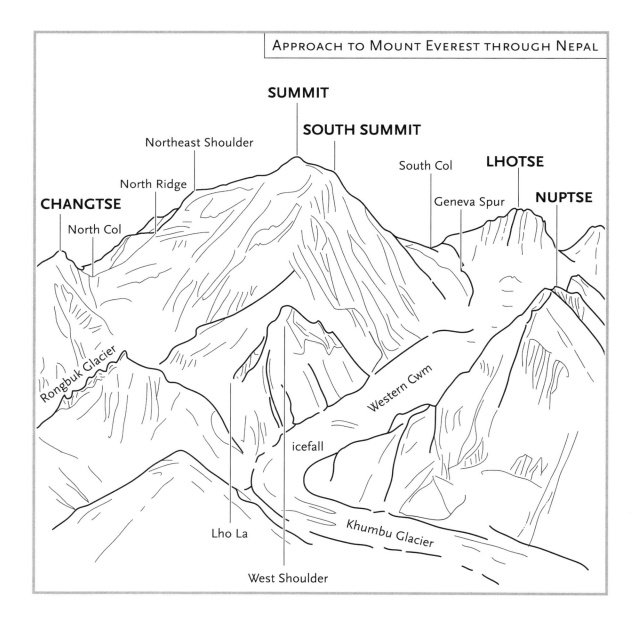

APPROACH TO MOUNT EVEREST THROUGH NEPAL

over the treacherous Khumbu Icefall. The strong climbing team, including New Zealander Edmund Hillary, determined that they could move through the icefall, and with this the expedition returned to Britain to prepare for another assault on Everest's summit.

But this was no longer the age of empire, and Britain no longer had a privileged position in South Asia. To the great shock of the British, the Nepalese government authorized a Swiss expedition to make an assault on Everest in 1952, under the auspices of the Swiss Foundation for Alpine Research. The British approached the Swiss about the possibility of staging a joint expedition, which the Swiss agreed to consider. During the ensuing negotiations, however, it became obvious that the British intended to take over this expedition and dictate terms to the Swiss, so the negotiations collapsed. With the British out of the picture, the Swiss appointed Ed Wyss-Dunant to lead their expedition. Wyss-Dunant then hired a Sherpa named Tenzing Norgay to be the *sirdar,* or head of the expedition's porters. Tenzing was 38 and had been to Everest with each of the British prewar expeditions. He had previously served as sirdar for two of the Swiss climbers on the 1952 expedition, André Roch and René Dittert, who regarded him with great respect and confidence. It was Tenzing and Raymond Lambert who made the expedition's final assault on Everest's summit in May 1952, after spending a night in their tent at 27,500 feet without sleeping bags and with virtually no food, melting snow over a candle to drink. They reached 28,210 feet before the bad weather turned them back.

The British mountaineers were greatly relieved that the Swiss had failed in their attempt to climb Everest. The Nepalese government had given them permission to make the next assault in 1953, and the British recognized that time was now of the essence. If they

failed in their ascent, the French would have the next opportunity to climb Everest in 1954, and then the Swiss again in 1955. Moreover, the British were keenly aware that the coronation of a new queen, Elizabeth II, would take place in June 1953. They were intent upon celebrating the coronation with the first successful ascent to the top of the world.

Under the leadership of John Hunt, a former officer in the Army of India, the expedition established its advanced base camp near the foot of the southwest face of the mountain. It then established a series of eight camps, before attempting a multistage assault on the summit. Two assault teams, and one team of porters, would ascend from Camp VIII. The first assault team of Charles Evans and Tom Bourdillon made their bid for the summit on May 26, closely followed by John Hunt and Da Namgyal, who carried supplies as far as they could for the second assault team of Edmund Hillary and Tenzing Norgay. As Evans and Bourdillon made their way toward the summit along the southeast ridge, Hunt and Namgyal reached the limit of their endurance and dropped their loads at 27,350 feet before retreating down the mountain. Evans and Bourdillon became the first to reach what is called the South Summit of Everest, which stands below the main peak. They attempted to push on, but due to intense fatigue and the late hour of the day, they were forced to turn back just several hundred feet short of their goal.

On May 28 the second assault team of Hillary and Tenzing set off toward the southeast ridge with the support team of George Lowe, Alf Gregory, and Ang Nyima. The five men picked up the supplies left by Hunt and Namgyal, adding them to their own loads. Hillary was now carrying more than 60 pounds, and each of the other men carried about 50 pounds as they proceeded to

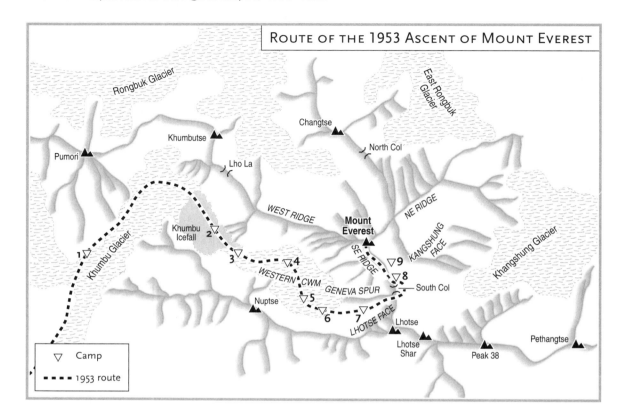

ROUTE OF THE 1953 ASCENT OF MOUNT EVEREST

27,900 feet, where they established Camp IX. All but Hillary and Tenzing returned down the mountain.

That night the two men ate chicken-noodle soup, canned apricots, and a hot lemon drink before going to sleep. They awoke at 4:00 A.M. and found the temperature to be minus 27 degrees Celsius. Hillary's boots were frozen, so he thawed them over their stove before attaching his crampons, a set of steel spikes that strap on to the soles of one's shoes for better traction on ice. Hillary and Tenzing then set off at 6:30 A.M. and were initially slowed by "breakable crust," a snow that has a thin, hard layer on top, through which the climber then breaks and falls with a jolt up to his or her knee or waist in soft snow

beneath. Fortunately, the terrain hardened as they reached the South Summit and then proceeded into a shallow saddle, from which they began their ascent of the peak along the summit ridge. Hillary went first, cutting steps into the icy snow, up which he and Tenzing climbed as a staircase toward the summit, which they could not yet see. Within just a few hundred feet of the summit, they came upon a rock face of about 40 feet that blocked their path. Hillary saw to the right of the rock face a large crack between the rock and a cornice, a large piece of ice hanging over a ridge. Hillary proposed to ascend through the crack, but there was a danger that the ice would break away from the rock, leaving him to fall thousands of feet down the face of the mountain.

Hillary moved into the crack, facing the rock. He describes his climb in his memoir, *View from the Summit:*

> I jammed my crampons into the ice behind me and then wriggled my way upward using every little handhold I could find. Puffing for breath, I made steady height—the ice was holding—and forty feet up I pulled

myself out of the crack onto the top of the rock face. I had made it!

With growing confidence, Hillary helped Tenzing to ascend through the crack. Hillary then used his ice axe to cut more steps upward. "Next moment I had moved onto a flattish exposed area of snow with nothing but space in every direction," Hillary recalls. "Tenzing

Tenzing Norgay (left) and Sir Edmund Hillary smile shortly after their 1953 ascent of Mount Everest, the summit of which is to the right of Hillary's head. *(Reuters/Landov)*

quickly joined me and we looked around in wonder. To our immense satisfaction, we realized we had reached the top of the world!" It was 11:30 A.M. Hillary extended his hand in a formal manner to his partner, but Tenzing declined to take Hillary's hand and instead gave him a strong bear hug in celebration. Hillary removed his oxygen mask, took out his camera and photographed Tenzing on the summit, holding his ice axe aloft with the flags of the United Nations, India, Nepal, and Great Britain fluttering in the stiff wind. Hillary then took pictures down every side of the mountain as proof of their achievement. Before they began their descent, Tenzing left bits of chocolate, cookies, and a pencil as gifts for the gods.

Epilogue
The Legacy of
Exploration and Empire

 European explorers in the so-called age of discovery had laid claim to the world in the name of their Christian God, seeking gold, silver, and spices to enhance the wealth and power of European monarchs. By contrast, in the modern era of exploration in Central Asia, Africa, and on the Arabian Peninsula, Christianity remained an important factor, but the pope no longer distributed the world's territories, and Christianity was now divided between Catholicism and Protestantism. Explorers sought raw materials and markets for the growing industrial economy of Europe, and they commonly preferred to let trade, rather than military campaigns, drive imperial expansion. Toward this end, Protestant missionaries played a prominent role in advocating the dual expansion of "Commerce and Christianity," condemning the conquistadores who had enslaved foreigners as heathen savages.

In the modern era, explorers recognized that the development of foreign markets required, not slavery, but wages for labor in a capitalist economy, wages that could then be spent on European goods. Modern explorers brought a scientific perspective to this search for commercial opportunities overseas, but the advancement of scientific knowledge also became an end in itself. The scientific nature of modern exploration reflected the influence of the intellectual movement known as the Enlightenment, but one should not presume that exploration was therefore more high-minded than before. As always, it commonly served to establish strategic advantages in the competition between European empires, whether on the Nile or in Tibet. The British Empire was the most powerful of the European overseas empires during most of the period between the 18th and 20th centuries, and it aggressively pursued exploration as a means to maintain its predominance.

CULTURES OF EMPIRE

Many events have intervened between the modern era of European exploration and the present day, but one can still see the explorers' many legacies. From the standpoint of the peoples of Central Asia, Africa, and the Arabian Peninsula, European exploration forged a path for the imperial conquests that quickly followed. Exploration, despite its noble promises, commonly gave way to economic exploitation and tremendous social and cultural upheaval. From the standpoint of Europe, however, exploration was a heroic and productive adventure. It changed the foods that Europeans ate, it located raw materials and markets that were crucial to Europe's industrial development, it provided many opportunities for employment, and it clearly became a source of national pride. Explorers became the subjects of children's books, in response to the rising literacy of the European public, and of music hall performances. They appeared on advertisements to sell everything from soap to medicine, their faces being instantly familiar to Europeans of every class.

Consider the differences between two of the great explorers of the early and modern eras of exploration. Christopher Columbus became estranged from the Spanish Crown in the last years of his life, and thus his death went unnoticed. He was buried without a single government official in attendance, unmourned by anyone beyond his family and friends. By contrast, when David Livingstone's body was returned to Britain from central Africa, he was buried in a state funeral among kings and queens in Westminster Abbey in London, a hero to the nation, rather than a servant beholden to a monarch.

EXPLORATION IN THE POST-IMPERIAL AGE

One might ask, Did exploration move beyond the so-called modern era and enter an altogether new era after the middle of the 20th century? The modern era of exploration was inextricably linked to European empires, which began to disintegrate after World War II. By the early 1960s, European empires across the globe were being displaced by new, independent nation states. There was arguably one exception to this: the transformation of the Russian Empire into the Soviet Union, which would not collapse until after 1989. The celebration of the conquest of Mount Everest in 1953, following the partition of British India into the nation states of India and Pakistan in 1947, offers a useful look as the impact of the process known as decolonization on a new era of exploration.

The leaders of the British expedition to Everest hoped to achieve their goal in time to declare their triumph before the coronation of Queen Elizabeth II in June 1953. They succeeded, and the conquest of Everest was announced in *The Times* of London on June 2, the day on which Elizabeth was crowned. *The Times* declared that this achievement was a "coronation gift" for the queen, and it observed that the same qualities that drove British explorers to success in the first Elizabethan Age (that is, in the 16th and early 17th centuries, when Elizabeth I was in power) were still alive. Despite this royal rhetoric, this was not, in fact, a return to the predominance of monarchs that one saw in the earlier era of European overseas exploration. The British monarchy had long ago been subordinated to the elected representatives of the people of Britain, and by 1953 the queen's coronation was a national, not just a royal, event. But neither of the men who reached the summit of Everest was British. Hillary was from New Zealand, and thus a member of the British Commonwealth, and Tenzing was from Nepal, though he had lived in Darjeeling, India, for many years. Of course, there had been previous explorers who were not citizens or sub-

Elizabeth II was crowned queen of Britain on June 2, 1953, the same day on which *The Times* of London announced that Sir Edmund Hillary and Tenzing Norgay had successfully reached the summit of Mount Everest. *(EPA/Landov)*

jects of the nations on behalf of whom they worked. Nonetheless, the presence of Tenzing on the summit of Everest introduced a new nationalist agenda to exploration, one that challenged the long-standing leadership of Europeans.

This challenge became apparent only during the celebration of the conquest of Everest, as the members of the expedition made their way home. As they approached Kathmandu, the capital of Nepal, Tenzing, Hillary, and Hunt were placed in a jeep. Nepali officials instructed Hillary and Hunt to sit, and they instructed Tenzing to stand, balancing him-

self upon the jeep's roll bar. They then proceeded into the capital, where Tenzing was cheered wildly as a national hero. To Hillary's annoyance, there were banners along the roads that pictured Tenzing atop Everest, holding his axe aloft in one hand, while holding a rope attached to a white man, who lay on his back with his feet and arms in the air. When King Tribhuvan introduced the three men to the people, he stated that Tenzing had reached the summit of Everest first. In fact, Hillary had led the way to the summit, but he and Tenzing had made a point of telling the king that they had arrived on the summit

With an interior space approximately equal to a three-bedroom house, the International Space Station has been operating since 2000. *(NASA)*

together. Subsequently, when the expedition arrived in Delhi, Tenzing was again hailed as the hero of the Everest climb, and he was identified as a resident of India in an attempt to garner his prestige for the Indian nation. When Tenzing and his family were invited to Britain, Indian prime minister Jawaharlal Nehru succeeded in giving Tenzing an

source of pride for non-Europeans who wished to mark their own achievements as independent nations.

While the national competition in exploration extended beyond Europe, another more cooperative and constructive development was marked by Tenzing's climb. One of the flags that he held aloft on his ice axe was the flag of the United Nations. He thus claimed the top of the world not only for particular nations but also for all humankind. The remarkable potential of international cooperation in exploration is now being demonstrated on another frontier, that of the planets and stars beyond earth. The International Space Station, the largest coordinated scientific undertaking in human history, is an exploratory mission like none other before it. Today exploration is identified, above all, with space, although there continue to be important explorations of the deep ocean floors, which remain largely unknown. In space exploration, which depends upon and contributes so much to scientific research, one can see an extension of the modern era of exploration. One certainly sees this in the quest for not only scientific knowledge but also commercial benefits, strategic advantages, and national prestige. Yet the future might offer a new era in exploration, when rockets, shuttles, and stations finally enable humans to settle in space. If that happens, it remains to be seen whether countries will make new claims to territory and, if these claims are made, how they will justify them. One wonders if space will be divided in the name of commerce, religion, or the nation. How this comes to pass may determine whether people have entered a new era of exploration after all.

Indian, rather than a Nepalese, passport. In the era of decolonization that followed World War II, exploration was no longer a triumphant story of European heroics, but a

GLOSSARY

abolitionist   An opponent of slavery.

bodhisattva   According to Buddhists, this is a person who has earned nirvana, but who has chosen to remain on earth in order to assist others in the quest for spiritual truth.

burgher   A former employee of the Dutch East India Company who established an independent farm near Cape Town, South Africa, after 1657.

calico   A simple, inexpensive cotton fabric.

Cathay   An ancient European name for the region of present-day China.

conquistador   A Spanish soldier.

cornice   An ice formation hanging over a ridge.

cowry   A seashell used as currency in Africa.

crampons   Steel spikes that attach to boots for better traction on ice.

Dalai Lama   The spiritual and political leader of Tibet.

dysentery   A potentially fatal disease of the intestines.

emir   A Muslim ruler in Central Asia.

ghazú   A Bedouin raiding party.

hajj   The Muslim pilgrimage to Mecca.

Iberian Peninsula   The region of present-day Spain and Portugal.

khan   A Muslim ruler in Central Asia.

Khoikhoi   Peoples of South Africa who lived in clans and supported themselves by herding cattle and fat-tailed sheep.

Moor   An ancient European term for a Muslim, generally from North Africa.

nirvana   According to Buddhists, this is the state of eternal tranquility that follows one's release from reincarnation.

palaver   An African term for negotiation.

papal dominion   The authority of the pope to determine sovereignty over land.

paraffin   A waxy substance used commonly to make candles.

pundit   A learned Indian who conducted surveys or other forms of exploration in the service of the British in India.

raja   A Hindu ruler in Asia.

Reconquista   The campaign by Christian monarchs to expel the Moors from the Iberian Peninsula. The Reconquista was ongoing between the eighth and late 15th centuries.

San   Peoples of South Africa who lived along the coast as hunter-gatherers.

Sherpas   A people of Tibetan origin who live primarily in the Khumbu region of Nepal.

sirdar   A leader among the porters of Himalayan climbs.

Tuareg   A Muslim marauder in the region of the Sahara Desert.

FURTHER INFORMATION

NONFICTION

Alder, Garry. *Beyond Bokhara: The Life of William Moorcroft.* London: Century Publishing, 1985.

Breashears, David, et al. *Last Climb: The Legendary Everest Expeditions of George Mallory.* New York: National Geographic, 1999.

Crosby, Alfred. *The Columbian Exchange.* New York: Praeger, 2003.

———. *Ecological Imperialism.* Cambridge: Cambridge University Press, 1993.

Curtin, Philip. *The World and the West.* Cambridge: Cambridge University Press, 2002.

———. *Disease and Empire.* Cambridge: Cambridge University Press, 1998.

———. *Image of Africa: British Ideas and Action, 1780–1850.* Madison: University of Wisconsin Press, 1973.

De Gramont, Sanche. *The Strong Brown God: The Story of the Niger River.* Boston: Houghton Mifflin Company, 1975.

Delpar, Helen. *The Discoverers: An Encyclopedia of Explorers and Exploration.* New York: McGraw-Hill Book Company, 1980.

Diamond, Jared. *Guns, Germs, and Steel.* New York: W. W. Norton & Co., 1999.

Farwell, Byron. *The Man Who Presumed: A Biography of Henry M. Stanley.* New York: W. W. Norton & Co., 1989.

Geniesse, Jane Fletcher. *Passionate Nomad: The Life of Freya Stark.* New York: Random House, 2001.

Headrick, Daniel. *The Tentacles of Progress.* New York: Oxford University Press, 1988.

Hillary, Edmund. *View from the Summit.* New York: Pocket Books, 1999.

Hopkirk, Peter. *Quest for Kim.* Ann Arbor: University of Michigan Press, 1999.

———. *The Great Game.* New York: Kodansha International, 1994.

———. *Trespassers on the Roof of the World.* London: John Murray, 1982.

Jeal, Tim. *Livingstone.* New Haven: Yale University Press, 2001.

Keay, John. *The Great Arc: The Dramatic Tale of How India Was Mapped and Everest Was Named.* New York: Perennial, 2000.

———. *The Gilgit Game: The Explorers of the Western Himalayas, 1865–95.* Oxford: Oxford University Press, 1993.

———. *When Men and Mountains Meet: The Explorers of the Western Himalayas, 1820–75.* Hamden, Conn.: Archon Books, 1982.

———. *The Mammoth Book of Explorers.* New York: Caroll & Graf, 2002.

———. *The Royal Geographical Society History of World Exploration.* London: Hamlyn, 1991.

Lewis, Bernard. *Cultures in Conflict.* New York: Oxford University Press, 1995.

McDonald, Bernadette. *Extreme Landscape: The Lure of Mountain Spaces.* New York: National Geographic, 2002.

McLynn, Frank. *Hearts of Darkness: The European Exploration of Africa.* New York: Carroll & Graf Publishers, 1992.

Moorehead, Alan. *The White Nile.* New York: Perennial, 2000.

———. *The Blue Nile.* New York: Perennial, 2000.

———. *The Fatal Impact: The Invasion of the South Pacific, 1767–1840.* New York: HarperCollins, 1990.

Morison, Samuel Eliot. *The Great Explorers: The European Discovery of America.* New York: Oxford University Press, 1986.

National Portrait Gallery. *David Livingstone and the Victorian Encounter with Africa.* London: National Portrait Gallery Publications, 1996.

Pakenham, Thomas. *The Scramble for Africa.* New York: Avon Books, 1992.

Parry, J. H. *The Age of Reconnaissance.* Berkeley: University of California Press, 1981.

Rice, Edward. *Captain Sir Richard Francis Burton: A Biography.* New York: DaCapo Press, 2001.

Roberts, David, and Jan Morris. *Great Exploration Hoaxes.* New York: Modern Library, 2001.

Shipman, Pat. *To the Heart of the Nile: Lady Florence Baker and the Exploration of Central Africa.* New York: Morrow, 2003.

Slung, Michele. *Living with Cannibals and Other Women's Adventures.* New York: National Geographic, 2001.

Sobel, Dava. *Longitude.* New York: Penguin USA, 1996.

Stark, Freya. *The Valleys of the Assassins.* New York: Modern Library, 2001.

Tenzing, Tashi. *Tenzing Norgay and the Sherpas of Everest.* Cambden, Me.: Ragged Mountain Press, 2001.

Thesiger, Wilfred. *Arabian Sands.* New York: Viking Press, 1981.

Tinling, Marion. *Women into the Unknown: A Sourcebook on Women Explorers and Travelers.* New York: Greenwood Press, 1989.

Unsworth, Walt. *Everest: The Mountaineering History.* Seattle: The Mountaineers, 2000.

FICTION

Kingsolver, Barbara. *The Poisonwood Bible.* New York: Perennial Press, 1999.

Kipling, Rudyard. *Kim.* New York: Viking Press, 1992.

Swift, Jonathan. *Gulliver's Travels.* New York: Penguin, 2003.

VHS/DVD

Great Adventurers: David Livingstone—Journey to the Heart of Africa (1999). Kultur Video, VHS, 1999.

Khartoum (1966). MGM/UA Video, DVD, 2002.

Lawrence of Arabia (1962). Columbia Tri-Star, VHS/DVD, 2001.

The Mission (1986). Warner Studios, VHS/DVD, 1995.

Mountains of the Moon (1990). Artisan Entertainment, VHS, 2002.

Nova: Lost on Everest (2000). WGBH Boston Video, VHS, 2000.

Stanley and Livingstone (1939). Twentieth Century Fox, VHS, 1990.

CD-ROM

Richard Burton's Arabian Nights and Victorian Books of Exploration and Travel in Asia and Africa. B & R Samizdat Express, 2002.

WEB SITES

Hakluyt Society. "Hakluyt Society Web Links Page." Available online. URL: www.hakluyt.com/haksoc-links.htm. Downloaded on 21 January 2004.

National Geographic Society. "Xpeditions." Available online. URL: www.nationalgeographic.com/expeditions/. Downloaded on January 21, 2004.

Peter McCracken. "Maritime History on the Internet." Available online. URL: ils.unc.edu/maritime/contact.shtml. Downloaded on January 21, 2004.

Royal Geographical Society. "Education Resources." Available online. URL: www.rgs.org/category. php?Page=mainarchives. Downloaded on January 21, 2004.

Society for the History of Discoveries. "Exploration and Cartography: Web Links." Available online. URL: www.sochistdisc.org/links.htm. Downloaded on January 21, 2004.

United States Library of Congress. "Geography and Map Reading Room." Available online. URL: www.loc.gov/rr/geogmap/gmpage.html. Downloaded on January 21, 2004.

United States Library of Congress. "Meeting of Frontiers." Available online. URL: frontiers.loc. gov/intldl/mtfhtml/mfsplash.html. Downloaded on January 21, 2004.

INDEX

Page numbers in *italics* indicate a photograph. Page numbers followed by *m* indicate maps. Page numbers followed by *g* indicate glossary entries. Page numbers in **boldface** indicate box features.